Far Inside The Arduino: Nano Every Supplement

by Tom Almy

Preface

Arduino has released the Arduino Nano Every board at a much lower price than the Arduino Nano board with claimed compatibility. This new board, as well as the Arduino Uno WiFi, use the much newer ATMega4809 microcontroller. This microcontroller has considerably more capability than the ATmega328P of the Arduino Nano and Uno, but the Arduino library hides this capability. For this reason this book was written.

Let's be upfront with what this book is not:
- It is not an education in basic electronics, programming, or even microcontrollers.
- It is not for people perfectly happy with the functionality of the Arduino Nano Every. There is no question that the Arduino library makes programming simpler.

When you start reading this book you are assumed to already have experience with the Arduino Uno or Nano (or equivalent clone) but also have the Arduino Nano Every board and are able to write, load, and run sketches. This book skips over the general descriptions of the interfaces (GPIO, SPI, USART,…) and concentrates on the specific implementation in the ATMega4809 and in particular how it differs from the ATmega328P in the Arduino Uno or Nano. The book *Far Inside The Arduino,* or equivalent, is recommended to gain this knowledge.

So then, what is this book about?
- It takes the features, usually expressed as function calls in the Arduino Library, and shows how they can be accessed directly in the AVR ATmega4809 microcontroller.
- It shows how to access most features that are hidden by the Arduino Library to keep things simple.

All peripheral interfaces are discussed — two-wire (TWI/I2C), SPI, USART, ADC, Analog Comparator, timer/counters and the basic Digital I/O, as well as the new Event System, Configurable Custom Logic, and other differing features. With this knowledge you can improve performance markedly, allowing larger, more sophisticated applications to be implemented, and obtain maximum value out of the Arduino Nano Every board.

Example programs can be downloaded from the author's website. See Source Code Available (page ?). In most cases only excerpts are in the book. The example programs are kept simple to show off the hardware features and make it easy to modify the programs for further explorations. They need few to no additional components. However an oscilloscope is needed to view the operation of some.

A few other things to get out of the way:

- "Pins" can refer to either the Arduino Nano Every board pins or the ATmega4809 pins. Which should be apparent by context.
- Arduino is being silly introducing new terminology. "Sketches" will be called "programs" in the remainder of this book.
- The "Arduino Programming Language" is just C++. The compiler is just the standard GCC compiler that targets the AVR microcontroller.
- Programs that run on microcontrollers are called "firmware" programs. However as far as this book is concerned, there is no real distinction between "firmware" and "software" so it will be called "software".
- The author will occasionally use the pronoun "I" when talking about his personal preferences or experiences.

Let's get started!

CONTENTS

CHAPTER ONE

Overview

The Arduino Nano Every is designed to mimic as closely as possible the functionality of the Arduino Nano, but using the more modern ATmega4809 microcontroller. This is unfortunate because the ATmega4809 has so much more to offer than the ATmega328P in the older Arduino Nano. Let's look at the major distinctions between the two. The older Nano values are in parenthesis.

- 6KB (2KB) RAM
- 48KB (32KB) Flash ROM (program memory)
- 320B (1024B) EEPROM (including "User Row")
- The program memory and the EEPROM are mapped into the data memory address space.
- Programmed via a new interface, UPDI, not requiring the USART. There is no longer boot loader code so all of the program memory is available to the application.
- USB interface chip changed to a SAM microcontroller from an AVR.
- Possible 20MHz (16MHz) operation. No longer uses or needs an external crystal.
- The Analog to Digital converter is capable of running up to 12 times faster, but runs at the same speed for compatibility.
- All the peripheral interfaces are of new designs, so function differently. The Arduino Library hides this.
- There is a delay of about 600ms between program loading and the availability of the USB USART (Serial Monitor in the IDE). This can cause characters written to the serial port to be lost if there is no delay before writing after program start.
- Arduino Nano Every is half the price of the Arduino Nano. However clones of the Nano are about a third of the price of the Arduino Nano Every. There are no clones of the Arduino Nano Every (yet).
- "Pin for pin compatible", but this isn't necessarily a good thing, nor is it quite true.
    - Nano Every is missing PWM (*analogWrite*) capability on D11.
    - All PWM output is 977Hz, or 1220Hz if clock speed increased to 20MHz.
    - Pins A6 and A7 can be used as digital I/O pins on the Nano Every.
    - SPI SS is on pin 8 on Nano Every, pin 10 on Nano.
    - External interrupts allowed on all pins, not just 2 and 3 (although readers of *Far Inside The Arduino* know about pin change interrupts

for all pins, it's just not part of the Arduino Library.)
- The USART on pins D0 and D1 is a separate USART from the one used to communicate over the USB connection.
- Minimum bit rate in the USART is 1200bps (300bps).

In order to maximize compatibility with the Nano, some capabilities of the ATmega4809 are effectively hidden.

- The Nano Every can be configured (by modifications to the board.txt file) to run at 20MHz, but is configured to run at 16MHz for compatibility, thus reducing performance by 20%.
- The board wastes two pins that could be used to bring out additional digital I/O pins. Instead one pin is unassigned and another is a duplicate of the reset pin.
- Digital pins 3, 6, 8, 11, 12, and 13 can also be used as inputs to the analog to digital converter (they are inputs 15, 14, 11, 8, 9, and 10, respectively) . In fact the analog pins 0 through 7 on the Nano Every don't connect to ADC inputs 0 through 7 respectively but to 3, 2, 1, 0, 12, 13, 4, and 5. You basically need a translation table and there are 14 (of 16) analog inputs actually available.
- There are four USARTs. The USB connected USART is USART3. This becomes unit *Serial* in the Arduino library. The serial port on pins 0 and 1 are USART1 on unit *Serial1*. The other two USARTs are not handled by the Arduino Library but exist on pins 2 (TX) and 7 (RX) for USART0 and pins 6 (TX) and 3 (RX) for USART2. To access USART2 requires changing a pin assignment.
- There is one "type A" 16-bit Timer/Counter. It has three compare channels which provide PWM on pins 5, 9, and 10 on channels 2, 0 and 1 respectively. It can be split into two 8-bit Timer/Counters each with three compare channels, however the additional three pins of PWM are not brought out on the board.
- There are four "type B" 16-bit Timer/Counters each of which runs as a 8-bit PWM generator. TCB0 provides PWM on pin 6 and TCB1 provides PWM on pin 3. The two other channel outputs are not accessible on the board. However TCB3 is used to implement the Arduino Library timer functions.

Features available but not used or presented by the Arduino library include: Timer/Counter input capture, dual-slope PWM on Type A Timer/Counter, 16-bit Real Time Counter and Programmable Interrupt Timer, Analog Comparator, Watchdog Timer, Event System, Configurable Custom Logic, sleep modes. All peripherals have additional features over those in the ATmega328P. Not all of the features are fully available because of pins not brought out on the board.

CHAPTER TWO

File Locations

It is frequently useful to look at source and header files of the Arduino library. The trick is finding them. For the Arduino Nano Every you must first add support for *Arduino megaAVR Boards* using the Boards Manager in the Arduino IDE. This installs the files needed to support the ATmega4809 and the Arduino Nano Every and Arduino Uno WiFi boards. These files are not installed in the same locations as the standard support files. In Windows 10 it is in (starting at your Home folder) *AppData\Local\Arduino15\packages\arduino*. Note that *AppData* is a hidden folder. On a Mac the new files can be found in *~/Library/Arduino15/packages/arduino*. In Linux it's *~/.Arduino15/packages/arduino*.

From this point *hardware/megaavr/1.8.5/libraries* contains the Arduino supplied libraries you can add to your programs.

hardware/megaavr/1.8.5/cores/arduino/ and the *api* subfolder contain the source files for the Arduino built-in functions. Here you can find every function and definition found on the Arduino website at https://www.arduino.cc/reference/en/. The organization and some of the file names are different than for the traditional Arduino board library.

Arduino.h — header file that is always included in Arduino programs.
api/binary.h — defines binary constants *B0* through *B11111111*.
UART* — USART drivers (serial ports).
main.cpp — the *main* function.
new.cpp — *new* and *delete* call *malloc* and *free*.
api/Print.* and **api/Printable.h** — implement the print function.
api/Stream.* — base class for streamable I/O
Tone.cpp — the *tone* function
api/WCharacter.h — Character functions like *isAlpha*
WInterrupts.c — *attachInterrupt* and *detachInterrupt*
wiring_analog.c — *analogRead* (ADC) and *analogWrite* (PWM).
wiring_digital.c — *digitalRead*, *digitalWrite*, and *pinMode*
wiring_pulse.* — *pulseIn*
wiring_shift.c — *shiftIn* and *shiftOut*
wiring.c — *init*, *millis*, *micros*, *delay*, and *delayMicroseconds*. *TCB3_INT* interrupt routine.
WMath.cpp — has random number functions, *map*, and *makeWord*.
api/String.* — String class.

hardware/megaavr/1.8.5/variants/nona4809/pins_arduino.h is used by the built-in functions and defines the capabilities of all the AVR pins. Also in this folder is *variant.c* which contains the function to configure the timers, and *timers.h* with some constant definitions for the timers.

tools/avr-gcc/7.3.0-atmel3.6.1-arduino5/avr/include/ contains the AVR include files. The standard C include files are here and there is an avr subfolder that contains the AVR specific additions. Particularly important is *avr/io.h* and *avr/iom4809.h*   for the definitions of all the I/O device registers, *avr/eeprom.h* for accessing eeprom, and *avr/ delay.h* for program delays.

AVR compiler tools are all in *hardware/tools/avr-gcc/7.3.0-atmel3.6.1-arduino5/bin*.

Note that all these locations have changed in the past and may change in the future. Arduino version 1.8.13 and Arduino megaAVR Boards 1.8.6 were used when writing this book.

CHAPTER THREE
Programming Issues and Clock Rate

Compatibility for pgmspace.h
It is no longer necessary to have specific coding practices for data in the program space. However existing code using PROGMEM and program memory accessing functions will continue to work as these keywords and functions refer to the conventional functions. When PROGMEM is used in the declaration the addresses are relative to the start of the program memory and not to the address space. This means that if PROGMEM is used the access functions must be used as well.

The example program *Nano_Every_Progmem* shows both using PROGMEM and not using PROGMEM for constant data storage. When run on the Nano Every, all the constant data is in program memory, with data declared PROGMEM having addresses relative to the start of program memory (0x4000). When run on an UNO or Nano, the data not declared PROGMEM is stored in RAM even though declared const.

Compatibility with Arduino Nano
There is a compatibility library provided that allows accessing the GPIO ports as though an Arduino Nano is being used. This can help in moving certain programs from the Arduino Nano to the Arduino Nano Every, however it won't work for programs using the Pins.h library I provided with the *Far Inside The Arduino* book. Instead use the revised Pins.h library provided with this book.

When compatibility mode is enabled, the file NANO_compat.h and NANO_compat.cpp are included. References to PORTB, PORTC, PORTD, DDRB, DDRC , and DDRD are cleverly modified to access the correct registers and bits in the ATmega4809. However the PIN registers are not included, nor is there compatibility for any other portions of the architecture. It is best not to use compatibility mode if you can avoid it.

Setting the clock speed
Earlier Arduino boards with AVR processors use a crystal to determine the clock speed. The ATmega4809 has an internal oscillator that is used. It can run at either a 16MHz or 20MHz clock speed with a simple change of a fuse bit when the part is programmed. To maintain compatibility with existing Arduino Nano programs the

speed is set at 16MHz. To run at 20MHz you can modify the boards.txt file.

To change the existing entry, you must first find it. It is called the nona4809. Change the line:
```
nona4809.build.f_cpu=16000000L
```
to:
```
nona4809.build.f_cpu=20000000L
```
and the line:
```
nona4809.bootloader.OSCCFG=0x01
```
to:
```
nona4809.bootloader.OSCCFG=0x02
```

As a more flexible alternative, add a new entry I call *fast4809*. Here is what it looks like. Note that because it may change in the future, use caution if you enter this directly into your file. This code is in the distribution as *AdditionToBoardsDotTxt.txt*.

```
fast4809.name=Arduino Fast Every

fast4809.vid.0=0x2341
fast4809.pid.0=0x0058

fast4809.upload.tool=avrdude
fast4809.upload.protocol=jtag2updi
fast4809.upload.maximum_size=49152
fast4809.upload.maximum_data_size=6144
fast4809.upload.speed=115200
fast4809.upload.use_1200bps_touch=true
fast4809.upload.extra_params=-P{serial.port}

fast4809.build.mcu=atmega4809
fast4809.build.f_cpu=20000000L
fast4809.build.board=AVR_NANO_EVERY
fast4809.build.core=arduino
fast4809.build.variant=nona4809
fast4809.build.text_section_start=.text=0x0
fast4809.build.extra_flags={build.328emulation} -DMILLIS_USE_TIMERB3
-DNO_EXTERNAL_I2C_PULLUP

fast4809.bootloader.tool=avrdude
fast4809.bootloader.file=atmega4809_uart_bl.hex
fast4809.bootloader.SYSCFG0=0xC9
fast4809.bootloader.BOOTEND=0x00
fast4809.bootloader.OSCCFG=0x02
fast4809.fuses.file=fuses_4809.bin

menu.mode=Registers emulation
fast4809.menu.mode.on=ATMEGA328
fast4809.menu.mode.on.build.328emulation=-DAVR_NANO_4809_328MODE
fast4809.menu.mode.off=None (ATMEGA4809)
```

```
fast4809.menu.mode.off.build.328emulation=
```

##

All the existing Arduino libraries base their timing on the value of *f_cpu* so should continue to run correctly. It is important that any code you write that has clock dependencies use the value of *f_cpu* if you intent your code to work at either clock speed.

Some speeds lower than 16MHz can also be set that use a clock divider in the microcontroller. Slower speeds do save power, but most people seem to want faster performance.

CHAPTER FOUR

Program Loading

Unlike other AVR based Arduino boards, the Arduino Nano Every has no bootloader and the full program memory is available for user programs. Instead programs are loaded using the UPDI, Unified Program and Debug Interface, that is built into the ATmega4809. The interface is a single dedicated pin on the microcontroller that communicates with a half-duplex UART protocol.

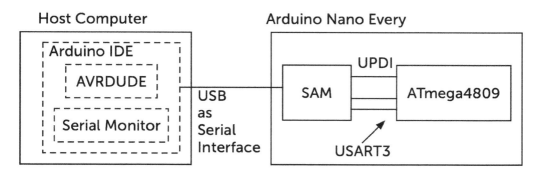

The SAM microcontroller in the Arduino provides the USB interface for both UPDI and USART3 (which is just the device *Serial* in the Arduino library). The UPDI commands originate from the AVRDUDE interface program running on the host computer via a command within the Arduino IDE. If there are no UPDI commands at reset, or when the last UPDI command is sent, the SAM switches over to driving USART3. This delay means that USART3 cannot be used immediately after boot-up and a delay is needed in the application program if it is using this interface.

The UPDI can reset the microcontroller, so the reset input of the microcontroller is not needed for operation of the Arduino Nano Every board. UPDI can also be used as a program debugger, however that capability is not implemented in the Arduino IDE software.

CHAPTER FIVE

Rosetta Stone

Here is the mapping of the Nano Every board pins to the ATmega4809 pins, and their functionality.

Board Pin, function	Microcontroller Pin, Port	Microcontroller Function
JP2-1, SCK, D13, LED	32, PE02	AIN10, SCK, EVOUTE
JP2-2, 3V3		
JP2-3, AREF (cap loaded)	27, PD07	AIN7, N2
JP2-4, A0	23, PD03	AIN3, N0, , CCL-LUT2-OUT
JP2-5, A1	22, PD02	AIN2, P0, EVOUTD, , CCL-LUT2-IN2
JP2-6, A2	21, PD01	AIN1, P3, , CCL-LUT2-IN1
JP2-7, A3	20, PD00	AIN0, CCL-LUT2-IN0
JP2-8, A4/SDA	46, PA02, 36, PF02	SDA (bonded), AIN12, EVOUTF, EVOUTA, CCL-LUT0-IN2, CCL-LUT3-IN2
JP2-9, A5/SCL	47, PA03, 37, PF03	SCL (bonded), AIN13, , CCL-LUT3-OUT
JP2-10, A6	24, PD04	AIN4, P1
JP2-11, A7	25, PD05	AIN5, N1
JP2-12, 5V	42, VDD, 28, AVDD	
JP2-13, RESETN	40, PF06	RESET
JP2-14, not connected		
JP2-15, VIN	no connection	
JP3-1, TX1 (D1)	16, PC04	TXD1
JP3-2, RX1 (D0)	17, PC05	RXD1
JP3-3, RESETN	40, PF06	RESET

JP3-4, GND	15, 29, 43 GND	
JP3-5, D2	44, PA00	TXD0, CCL-LUT0-IN0
JP3-6, D3~	39, PF05	AIN15, RXD2, TCB1-WO
JP3-7, D4	18, PC06	
JP3-8, D5~	6, PB02	TCA0-WO2, EVOUTB
JP3-9, D6~	38, PF04	AIN14, TXD2, TCB0-WO
JP3-10, D7	45, PA01	RXD0, , CCL-LUT0-IN1
JP3-11, D8	33, PE03	AIN11, SS
JP3-12, D9~	4, PB00	TCA0-WO0
JP3-13, D10~	5, PB01	TCA0-WO1
JP3-14, MOSI, D11	30, PE00	AIN8, MOSI
JP3-15, MISO, D12	31, PE01	AIN9, MISO
TX of SAM, "RX0"	9, PB05	RXD3
RX of SAM, "TX0"	8, PB04	TXD3

Function descriptions: AINn - ADC input n, Nn Pn - analog comparator input n, TXDn RXDn — USART n, EVOUTn - Event Output n, CCL - Configurable Custom Logic, TCA0-WOn - Timer Counter A 0 Waveform Out n, TCBn-WO - Timer Counter Bn Waveform Out, SDA SCL - I2C/TWI interface, SCK MISO MOSI SS - SPI interface. RESET is reset function input (active low).

While the digital GPIO pins on the board are marked with a leading "D", sometimes they are just identified by the number. So, for instance "D2" and "2" refer to the same board pin.

Port pins not connected: PA04, PA05, PA06, PA07, PB03, PC00, PC01, PC02, PC03, PC07, PD06, PF00, PF01. Maybe someday there will be a board that brings these out.

Board pins A4 and A5 are each connected to two microcontroller pins (PA02/PF02 and PA03/PF03 respectively). It is important that if they are used as digital outputs, only one of the pair of pins is driven. The Arduino library uses PF02 and PF03, which are the port pins for the ADC. However PA02 and PA03 are the pins for TWI SDA and SCL respectively. So the TWI and ADC inputs A4 or A5 cannot be used simultaneously.

Port assignment is used to get non-default assignment of TXD1/RXD1, TXD3/RXD3, SPI, TWI, and the Timer/Counters. To access USART2 (TXD2/RXD2) requires manually changing the port assignment from inaccessible pins to D6 and D3. This can be done with the statement:

```
PORTMUX.USARTROUTEA |= PORTMUX_USART2_ALT1_gc;
```

Not all timer counter outputs are available, nor all the pins for synchronous USART operation. Also the USART unit numbers and ADC input numbers of the microcontroller are not the same as that of the Arduino firmware and board markings.

CHAPTER SIX

Memory Organization

While still maintaining the Harvard architecture of other AVR microcontrollers, the ATmega4809 mirrors the program memory in the data memory address space making it easy to access data stored in program memory. Any data defined with the *const* keyword will be stored in program memory. There is no need to use the PROGMEM keyword and the data can be accessed exactly like data in RAM.

The EEPROM is also readable in the data space but must still be written using function calls. There is 256 bytes of EEPROM plus an additional 64 bytes within the Nonvolatile Memory address space called the User Row. The User Row is not erased as part of a chip erase, which is generally not an issue as in the Arduino IDE the EEPROM is not erased or written with program loading.

Note that unlike other AVRs, most CPU registers are not part of the data address space. In fact only the stack pointer and status registers can be accessed and they are in the low data address space. They are named CPU_SPH (high byte), CPU_SPL (low byte), and CPU_SREG. These also go by the synonymous names SPH, SPL, and SREG. There is an additional new CPU register called the Configuration Change Protection register. This register is in the low address space and goes by the name CPU_CCP or just CCP.

ATmega4809 Data Address Space

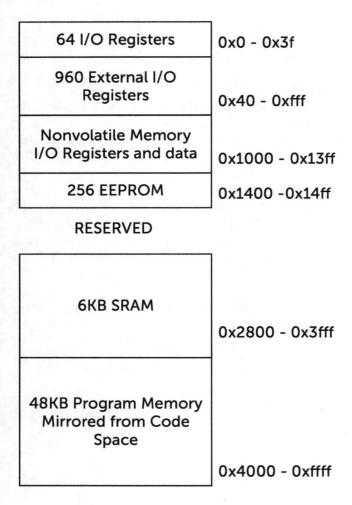

64 I/O Registers	0x0 - 0x3f
960 External I/O Registers	0x40 - 0xfff
Nonvolatile Memory I/O Registers and data	0x1000 - 0x13ff
256 EEPROM	0x1400 - 0x14ff

RESERVED

6KB SRAM	0x2800 - 0x3fff
48KB Program Memory Mirrored from Code Space	0x4000 - 0xffff

As in other AVRs, memory locations 0 through 0x3f are "low address space" and can be easily accessed with the CPU IN and OUT instructions, so are desirable I/O register addresses. The ATmega4809 makes good use of these by mirroring the most commonly used I/O registers that are in "External" address range into some of these low address locations. Four of these locations are called General Purpose I/O registers and are available for use as global variables or flags. They can be accessed as GPIOR0 through GPIOR3.

The AVR library groups most I/O registers into C++ structs. This is very convenient for GPIO register independent code, such as in the Arduino Wire library and to make code that is specific interface independent, such as in implementing code for all four

USARTs where a pointer to the USART register struct is used rather than the specific registers themselves.

Let's use this register as an example:

Control C Register USARTn.CTRLC

Bit	7	6	5	4	3	2	1	0
	CMODE1	CMODE0	PMODE1	PMODE0	SBMODE	CHSIZE2	CHSIZE1	CHSIZE0

Most registers can either be accessed using the structure name for the module they are in, such as USART0.CTRLC, or via the directly named register, which would be USART0_CTRLC. The generated code will be the same, so there is no advantage to using the direct name.

Most register fields are named as well, using #*define* or *enum*. Field values are named with a trailing _*gc*. The values are always shifted to the correct bits in the register. As an example, the value for even parity mode in the 2-bit PMODE field of USART0.CTRLC is named *USART_PMODE_EVEN_gc* and has the value (0x02<<4), the value being two shifted left four bits. Groups of bits, such as the PMODE field, have names for the bit mask ending in _*gm*, *USART_PMODE_gm*, which in this case has the value 0x30, and a name for the position ending in _*gp*, *USART_PMODE_gp*, which in this case has the value 4. Single bits may also be named, ending with _*bm* for the mask and _*bp* for the position. In this case there are *USART_PMODE0_bm* and *USART_PMODE0_bp* for the least significant bit of the field and *USART_PMODE1_bm* and *USART_PMODE1_bp* for the most significant bit.

The *avr/iom4809.h* file should be kept handy to reference all the names. This book shows only some of the names in the examples.

CHAPTER SEVEN

EEPROM

Because the EEPROM is mapped into the memory address space, contents can be read without needing a function call. However EEPROM locations still must be written via function calls. There is a 256 byte block of EEPROM, however there is an additional 64 bytes of EEPROM referred to as USERROW. The USERROW is not erased when the chip is erased. The Arduino IDE normally does not erase any EEPROM when loading programs, but other developer software might do so. It depends on the setting of a fuse bit.

For reading, the EEPROM starts at memory location 0x1400. The USERROW starts at location 0x1300. Symbols are defined for this: EEPROM_START for the starting address of the EEPROM and USER_SIGNATURES_START for the start of the USERROW.

To write to EEPROM include *<avr/eeprom.h>* and use the functions *eeprom_write_byte*, *eeprom_write_word*, *eeprom_write_dword*, *eeprom_write_float*, or *eeprom_write_block*. These are the same as used with the ATmega328P. Using these functions, we consider EEPROM to start at location 0 and the USERROW to start at location 0xff00, 256 bytes before location 0.

The following declaration defines a structure for the EEPROM called MYEEPROM. In this example the EEPROM contains a byte and two word values, with the remaining locations unused.

```
struct MYEEPROM {
  byte aByte;
  word aWord;
  word aSecondWord;
} * const foo = (struct MYEEPROM *) EEPROM_START;
// Write location is relative to start of EEPROM
// Read location is mapped into address space
#define eeprom_w  (* (struct MYEEPROM *) 0)
#define eeprom    (* (struct MYEEPROM *) EEPROM_START)
```

To access a value, say that of *aWord*, we can use *eeprom.aWord* or *foo->aWord*. I find the former nicer to use, but they are identical in generated code. We must use the functions to write to the EEPROM. For example, *eeprom_write_word(&eeprom_w.aWord, 1234);*

The USERROW can be declared similarly.

```
struct MYUSERROW {
  byte aByte;
  word aWord;
  word anArray[10];
};
// User Row is -256 bytes before the start of EEPROM
#define userrow_w (* (struct MYUSERROW *)0xFF00)
#define userrow (* (struct MYUSERROW *) USER_SIGNATURES_START)
```

An example of both the EEPROM and the USERROW are in the provided example program *eeprom_test*.

CHAPTER EIGHT

Interrupts

The ATmega4809 has additional interrupt configuration features to alter the priority of interrupts. Normally the interrupt priority is as shown in the list, below. If two or more interrupts are being requested, the one with the highest priority will be serviced first.

If an address of an interrupt vector is stored in CPUINT.LVL1VEC, that interrupt will be raised to a higher priority than any of the other interrupts, except for the non-maskable interrupts which are always highest priority. The Arduino library uses this feature in its USART code to temporarily raise the priority so that USART interrupts can occur within an interrupt routine trying to write to the USART port.

Round robin scheduling can be enabled by setting CPUINT.CTRLA bit CPUINT_LVL0RR_bm. When this is done the vector table becomes circular, with the highest priority vector being the one below the interrupt last serviced, and the first maskable interrupt in the table being below the priority of the last in the table. While this would seem to be a good way to insure all interrupts are serviced, the reality is that if there is insufficient performance to service all interrupts with regular scheduling, that would most likely still be true for round robin scheduling.

The interrupt vectors are listed below in decreasing priority order. Those interrupts used in the Arduino library are indicated.

Vector 0 is the reset vector, and is non-maskable.
CRCSCAN_NMI — Optional CRC scan of memory failed. This is also a non-maskable interrupt.

BOD_VLM — Brown Out Detect Voltage Level Monitor. "Early warning".

RTC_CNT — Real Time Counter interrupt, for overflow or counter match.
RTC_PIT — Real Time Counter Periodic Interrupt Timer interrupt.

CCL_CCL — Configurable Custom Logic interrupt

PORTA_PORT — External Interrupt on PORTA, used by *attachInterrupt*()

TCA0_OVF — Timer/Counter A overflow

TCA0_HUNF — Timer/Counter A underflow (split mode)
TCA0_CMP0 — Timer/Counter A compare 0 match
TCA0_CMP1 — Timer/Counter A compare 1 match
TCA0_CMP2 — Timer/Counter A compare 2 match

TCB0_INT — Timer/Counter B0 interrupt

TCB1_INT — Timer/Counter B1 interrupt, used by *tone*() function.

TWI0_TWIS — TWI Slave interrupt, used by Arduino TWI functions.
TWI0_TWIM — TWI Master interrupt, used by Arduino TWI functions.

SPI0_INT — SPI interrupt

USART0_RXC — USART 0 Receive Complete
USART0_DRE — USART 0 (Transmit) Data Register Empty
USART0_TXC — USART 0 Transmit Complete

PORTD_PORT — External Interrupt on PORTD, used by *attachInterrupt*()

AC0_AC — Analog Comparator interrupt

ADC0_RESRDY — ADC Result Ready
ADC0_WCOMP — ADC Window Compare

PORTC_PORT — External Interrupt on PORTC, used by *attachInterrupt*()

TCB2_INT — Timer/Counter B2 interrupt, used by the Servo library

USART1_RXC — USART 1 Receive Complete, used by *Serial1* UART interface
USART1_DRE — USART 1 (Transmit) Data Register Empty, used by *Serial1* UART interface
USART1_TXC — USART 1 Transmit Complete

PORTF_PORT — External Interrupt on PORTF, used by *attachInterrupt*()

NVMCTRL_EE — EEPROM Write/Erase Ready

USART2_RXC — USART 2 Receive Complete
USART2_DRE — USART 2 (Transmit) Data Register Empty
USART2_TXC — USART 2 Transmit Complete

PORTB_PORT — External Interrupt on PORTB, used by *attachInterrupt*()

PORTE_PORT — External Interrupt on PORTE, used by *attachInterrupt()*

TCB3_INT — Timer/Counter B3 interrupt, always used by Arduino library, time tracking functions.

USART3_RXC — USART 3 Receive Complete, used by *Serial* UART interface (connected to USB)

USART3_DRE — USART 3 (Transmit) Data Register Empty, used by *Serial* UART interface

USART3_TXC — USART 3 Transmit Complete

CHAPTER NINE

Event System

The *Event System* in the ATmega4809 provides the means to connect events or signals on one peripheral device to action triggers on one or more other peripheral devices. The events are mostly the signals that can cause interrupts. These are called *event generators*. The actions are such things as input capture in timer/counters, triggers to start an ADC measurement, or the driving of a digital pin. The actions are called *event users*.

The connection between event generators and users are over *event channels*. There are eight event channels, numbered 0 through 7. Each event channel can be connected to a single event generator source, however in the case of port pins and the Periodic Interrupt Timer only certain channels can be used for the specific source. There are 24 event users, each of which can be connected to one of the event channels. More than one event user can be connected to an event channel.

Event Generators

The following event generators are available with the symbolic name for the channel value as shown. The values are stored in EVSYS.CHANNEL0 through EVSYS.CHANNEL7. A value of 0 (EVSYS_GENERATOR_OFF_gc) turns the channel off.

- UPDI SYNC character (EVSYS_GENERATOR_UPDI_gc)
- RTC Overflow (EVSYS_GENERATOR_RTC_OVF_gc)
- RTC Compare Match (EVSYS_GENERATOR_RTC_CMP_gc)
- PIT prescaled clock (EVSYS_GENERATOR_RTC_PITn_gc, see below)
- CCL LUTn output (asynchronous) (EVSYS_GENERATOR_CCL_LUTn_gc) n=0,1,2,3
- AC comparator output (asynch) (EVSYS_GENERATOR_AC0_OUT_gc)
- ADC result ready (EVSYS_GENERATOR_ADC0_COMP_gc)
- PORT pin input (asynchronous) (EVSYS_GENERATOR_PORTn_PINm_gc, see below)
- USARTn baud clock (EVSYS_GENERATOR_USARTn_XCK_gc) n=0,1,2,3
- SPI SPI master clock (SCK) (EVSYS_GENERATOR_SPI0_SCK_gc)
- TCA Overflow (EVSYS_GENERATOR_TCA0_OVF_LUNF_gc)
- TCA Underflow in split mode (EVSYS_GENERATOR_TCA0_HUNF_gc)
- TCA Compare match channel n (EVSYS_GENERATOR_TCA0_CMPn_gc) n=0,1,2

- TCB*n* CAPT interrupt flag set (EVSYS_GENERATOR_TCB*n*_CMP0_gc) *n=0,1,2,3*

All event generators are available for every channel but for the PIT clock and PORT pins.

For the PIT clock different clock dividers are accessible as PIT0 through PIT3 depending on the channel:

Input	Channels 0, 2, 4, 6	Channels 1, 3, 5, 7
PIT0	/8192	/512
PIT1	/4096	/256
PIT2	/2048	/128
PIT3	/1024	/64

For the PORT pins, the actual port depends on the channel. Channels 6 and 7 are not used.

Input (*n*=0 through 7)	Channels 0, 1	Channels 2,3	Channels 4,5
PORT0_PIN*n*	Port A Pin *n*	Port C Pin *n*	Port E Pin *n*
PORT1_PIN*n*	Port B Pin *n*	Port D Pin *n*	Port F Pin *n*

So, for example, to connect Arduino Digital pin 2 to channel 0, we would look up and see that pin 2 is Port A pin 0. That would be PORT0_PIN0. We could use channel 1 instead, but those are the only two that could be used. The configuration statement would be:

```
EVSYS.CHANNEL0 = EVSYS_GENERATOR_PORT0_PIN0_gc;
```

It is also possible to generate events in software. By writing a "1" to the corresponding bit in the EVSYS.STROBE register, a single event is generated immediately. The register is defined:

Bit	7	6	5	4	3	2	1	0
Function	Chan 7	Chan 6	Chan 5	Chan 4	Chan 3	Chan 2	Chan 1	Chan 0

There are constant masks defined for each of these,
EVSYS_STROBE0_EV_STROBE_CH*n*_gc for *n*=0 through 7.

Event Users

There are registers for each of the event users, defined in the EVSYS structure. The register value is one plus the event generator to connect to. This way a value of zero represents "off". There are constants defined for this — EVSYS_CHANNEL_OFF_gc, EVSYS_CHANNEL_CHANNEL0_gc through EVSYS_CHANNEL_CHANNEL7_gc.

A single channel can be assigned to more than one user. The event users are:
- USERCCLLUT0A CCL LUT0 event input A
- USERCCLLUT0B CCL LUT0 event input B
- USERCCLLUT1A CCL LUT1 event input A
- USERCCLLUT1B CCL LUT1 event input B
- USERCCLLUT2A CCL LUT2 event input A
- USERCCLLUT2B CCL LUT2 event input B
- USERCCLLUT3A CCL LUT3 event input A
- USERCCLLUT3B CCL LUT4 event input B
- USERADC0 Trigger the ADC measurement
- USEREVOUTA EVSYS pin output A (Arduino A4)
- USEREVOUTB EVSYS pin output B (Arduino D5)
- USEREVOUTC EVSYS pin output C (not accessible - Port C Pin 2)
- USEREVOUTD EVSYS pin output D (Arduino A1)
- USEREVOUTE EVSYS pin output E (Arduino D13)
- USEREVOUTF EVSYS pin output F (Arduino A4, same as output A)
- USERUSART0 USART 0 event input
- USERUSART1 USART 1 event input
- USERUSART2 USART 2 event input
- USERUSART3 USART 3 event input
- USERTCA0 TCA event input
- USERTCB0 TCB0 event input
- USERTCB1 TCB1 event input
- USERTCB2 TCB2 event input
- USERTCB3 TCB3 event input

So, for example, to configure the TCB0 event input on channel 0 we would execute:
```
EVSYS.USERTCB0 = EVSYS_CHANNEL_CHANNEL0_gc;
```

Examples of use will be given in later chapters of this book.

CHAPTER TEN

Port Multiplexer

The Port Multiplexer allows the assignment of the internal peripheral devices to alternative pins. This is useful because the part is basically pin limited. In the case of the Arduino Nano Every, this facility is used in several cases because alternate assignments are necessary. These assignments are reflected in the section Chapter Five - Rosetta Stone (page 10). In addition to the Port Multiplexer, a fuse bit determines if the RESET pin acts as a reset or as a GPIO Pin PF6. The Arduino software configures this as a RESET pin however it can be changed as described in the next section Chapter Eleven - GPIO (page 29).

PORTMUX.EVSYSROUTEA

This register controls the routing of EVOUTA through EVOUTF to pins. The Event System is not used by the Arduino library. However, there is no reason to change this from the default value of 0.

PORTMUX.CCLROUTEA

This register controls the routing the configurable custom logic. Configurable Custom Logic is not used by the Arduino library. However, there is no need to change this from the default value of 0.

PORTMUX.USARTROUTEA

USART1, USART2, and USART3 require using the alternate pin assignments. The alternate assignment for USART3 is done when *Serial* is used and the alternate assignment for USART1 is made when *Serial1* is used. If USART2 is used, or if USART1 or USART3 are used without the Arduino Serial driver, then they must be assigned alternate pins in the application. All of them can be configured with the single statement:

```
PORTMUX.USARTROUTEA = PORTMUX_USART1_ALT1_gc |
                      PORTMUX_USART2_ALT1_gc |
                      PORTMUX_USART3_ALT1_gc;
```

PORTMUX.TWISPIROUTEA

The SPI requires using alternate pin assignment. The alternate assignment is made when the SPI library is used. When writing code for this interface directly it must be assigned alternate pins in the application. This can be configured with:

```
PORTMUX.TWISPIROUTEA = PORTMUX_SPI0_ALT2_gc;
```

In theory, the TWI would require alternate pin assignments as well when using separate pins for master and slave. However the board connects them together ("bonded") so using the alternate assignment for dual mode operation would offer no benefit.

PORTMUX.TCAROUTEA

TCA pins can be put on any port. For the Arduino Nano Every, they must be on Port B. The Arduino initialization code does this with:

```
PORTMUX.TCAROUTEA  = PORTMUX_TCA0_PORTB_gc;
```

PORTMUX.TCBROUTEA

There are alternative pins for each TCB output. For the Arduino Nano Every, the alternate pins for TCB0 (PF4) and TCB1 (PF5) must be used. TCB2 and TCB3 are not accessible on the Arduino pins. The Arduino initiation code does this with:

```
PORTMUX.TCBROUTEA = PORTMUX_TCB0_bm | PORTMUX_TCB1_bm;
```

CHAPTER ELEVEN

GPIO

IMPORTANT NOTE: *Be sure Register Emulation in the Arduino IDE is set to "NONE (ATMEGA4809)" when using any of the registers described in this section!*

The GPIO interface is considerably different from that in the ATmega328P microcontroller. There are 6 ports, labeled A through F. All ports are 8 bits except for port B with 6 bits, E with 4 bits, and F with 7 bits. Even though there are 41 GPIO pins, only 22 are accessible on the Arduino Nano Every board and the Arduino library. Peripheral functions usually override GPIO pins, and the ADC also uses pins of port D, port E, and port F bits 2 through 5.

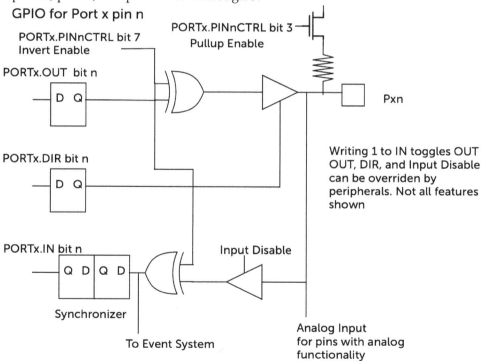

The ATmega4809 header file organizes I/O registers by module and puts all the registers in C++ structs. The older AVR microcontrollers have a flat organization. For instance, take the Data Direction register for port B. In the ATmega328P this is simply defined:

```
#define DDRB _SFR_IO8(0x04)
```

This puts the register at location 0x04. In the ATmega4809, all the registers of PORTB are defined as an instance of struct PORT_t at location 0x0420:

```
#define PORTB                    (*(PORT_t *) 0x0420) /* I/O Ports */
```

But this structure contains multiple registers, of course. The structure is defined:

```
typedef struct PORT_struct
  {
    register8_t DIR;    /* Data Direction */
    register8_t DIRSET;   /* Data Direction Set */
    register8_t DIRCLR;   /* Data Direction Clear */
    register8_t DIRTGL;   /* Data Direction Toggle *
    register8_t OUT;   /* Output Value */
    register8_t OUTSET;   /* Output Value Set */
    register8_t OUTCLR;   /* Output Value Clear */
    register8_t OUTTGL;   /* Output Value Toggle */
    register8_t IN;   /* Input Value */
    register8_t INTFLAGS;   /* Interrupt Flags */
    register8_t PORTCTRL;   /* Port Control */
    register8_t reserved_0x0B;
    register8_t reserved_0x0C;
    register8_t reserved_0x0D;
    register8_t reserved_0x0E;
    register8_t reserved_0x0F;
    register8_t PIN0CTRL;   /* Pin 0 Control */
    register8_t PIN1CTRL;   /* Pin 1 Control */
    register8_t PIN2CTRL;   /* Pin 2 Control */
    register8_t PIN3CTRL;   /* Pin 3 Control */
    register8_t PIN4CTRL;   /* Pin 4 Control */
    register8_t PIN5CTRL;   /* Pin 5 Control */
    register8_t PIN6CTRL;   /* Pin 6 Control */
    register8_t PIN7CTRL;   /* Pin 7 Control */
    register8_t reserved_0x18;
    register8_t reserved_0x19;
    register8_t reserved_0x1A;
    register8_t reserved_0x1B;
    register8_t reserved_0x1C;
    register8_t reserved_0x1D;
    register8_t reserved_0x1E;
    register8_t reserved_0x1F;
    register8_t reserved_0x1F;
  } PORT_t;
```

So instead of writing DDRB |= 1<<2; one would write PORTB.DIR |= 1<<2;

However, I would guess as a concession to the traditionalists, they have also defined:
`#define PORTB_DIR  _SFR_MEM8(0x0420)`
So one can avoid the structure and write `PORTB_DIR |= 1<<2;`

Compared to the older AVR microcontrollers, the DIR register is the older DDR register, the IN register is the older PIN register, and the OUT register is the older PORT register. However writing to the OUT register when the pin is configured as an input does not enable or disable the pullup. This is now done via the PINnCTRL registers. Writing to the IN register when the pin is configured as an output will toggle the pin like writing to the PIN register did. You can get the same result by writing to the OUTTGL register.

Note that the Arduino Library's digitalWrite will enable or disable the pullup when the pin is configured as an input. This is done to achieve compatibility with the older Arduino AVR boards.

Virtual Ports

The Virtual Port feature duplicates the most commonly accessed port registers, DIR, OUT, IN, and INTFLAGS into the bit-accessible lower addresses. This gives us smaller and slightly faster code and also accesses the registers atomically (a single read-modify-write access). We would do `VPORTB.DIR |= 1<<2;`

There is a VPORT for each port, A through F. The structure definition is:
```
typedef struct VPORT_struct
{
    register8_t DIR;   /* Data Direction */
    register8_t OUT;   /* Output Value */
    register8_t IN;  /* Input Value */
    register8_t INTFLAGS;  /* Interrupt Flags */
} VPORT_t;
```

They have also added what I call virtual registers in the PORT structure that are write only and modify an existing register. DIRSET will set bits in the DIR register eliminating the need to read the register first. So `PORTB.DIRSET = 1<<2;` That means that the read-modify-write is not necessary, however it is still at a larger address meaning a less efficient instruction than using VPORTB. Both DIR and OUT have SET, CLR, and TGL (set, clear, and toggle) virtual registers to eliminate needing read-modify-write.

I've revised the Pins library provided in *Far Inside The Arduino* to handle the new structure of the ATmega4809. Using this library we can still write `ddr.digital_5 = 1;` to change digital pin 5 (Port B bit 2 on the Arduino Nano Every) to be an output pin. This library defines dir, pin, port, and intflg to access the VPORT registers DIR, IN, OUT, and INTFLAGS.

There are new registers for pin and port control and interrupt enables.

Pin Control Registers

Every port pin has a control register. Port x pin n will be PORTx.PINnCTRL. For instance digital pin 2, which is port A pin 0 has the control register PORTA.PIN0CTRL.

Port Pin Control Register PORTx.PINnCTRL

Bit	7	6	5	4	3	2	1	0
Function	INVEN				PULLUPEN	ISC		

The *INVEN* bit is new functionality not in the older ATmega328P. If this bit is set then the external pin is inverted for both input and output. This provides a clever way to have active low pins while programming as though they are active high. We would invert digital pin 2 with:

```
PORTA.PIN0CTRL |= 1<<PORT_INVEN_bp;
```

Pullup enable functionality is now controlled by the *PULLUPEN* bit, rather than by the value in the PORT/OUT register. While not as convenient (as you must find the correct pin control register for the Arduino pin) this provides better functionality as the pullup enable state remains unchanged when using the pin for bidirectional applications. Thus there is no third output state that is passed through to go from tri-state (open) to driven high or from pull-up input to driven low. You just set the OUT register and then change the pin direction to output. So we would enable the pullup on digital pin 2 with:

```
PORTA.PIN0CTRL |= 1<<PORT_PULLUPEN_bp;
```

The ISC, input sense configuration, bits can be used to disable the input buffer (which *should* be done for pins used for analog inputs or unused pins) and also set the condition which will cause an interrupt. The values are:

Value	Name	Description
0	PORT_ISC_INTDISABLE_gc	Enabled digital input, no interrupt
1	PORT_ISC_BOTHEDGES_gc	Interrupt on both edges
2	PORT_ISC_RISING_gc	Interrupt on rising edge
3	PORT_ISC_FALLING_gc	Interrupt on falling edge
4	PORT_ISC_INPUT_DISABLE_gc	Digital input buffer and interrupt disabled
5	PORT_ISC_LEVEL_gc	Interrupt on low level
6 or 7		Reserved, undefined

It is important to note that if LEVEL is selected then the interrupt will occur repeatedly as long as the level is low. This is probably not what you want!

Each port has a port control register, PORTCTRL. The least significant bit limits the slew rate for all pins in the port. No other bits in that register are used.

Interrupts

Each port has an interrupt vector associated with it, PORTA_PORT through PORTF_PORT. Each port also has an interrupt flag register, PORTx.INTFLAGS or VPORTx.INTFLAGS for the virtual port. When a change on a port pin causes an interrupt based on the ISC bits for the pin, the corresponding bit in INTFLAGS is set and an interrupt is requested. The interrupt service routine must check INTFLAGS to see which pin or pins are causing the interrupt, and then must clear the flag bit as the only way the bit gets cleared is via software. As usual, the flag bit is cleared by writing a "1" to it. Clearing the flag bit should be done as an atomic operation by using the VPORT INTFLAGS register. The interrupt service routine may be exited when all INTFLAGS have been examined and cleared. If the service routine returns without clearing a flag, the routine will execute again.

The provided example program *interupt_test* illustrates port pin interrupts and digital I/O. A square wave on pin 3, generated with the *analogWrite* function, causes an interrupt on both edges. Pin 3 is Port F bit 5. Pins 4 and 5 are configured as outputs. The *Pins.h* library is used to define and easily access the pins. An oscilloscope is connect to observe all three pins. The setup function is:

```
#include <Pins.h>
void setup() {
  analogWrite(3, 128); // Put a square wave on pin 3, PF05
  ddr.digital_4 = 1; // Set pins 4 and 5 as outputs.
  ddr.digital_5 = 1;
  PORTF.PIN5CTRL |= PORT_ISC_BOTHEDGES_gc; // interrupt on both
                                           // edges of PF5
}
```

On the rising edge of pin 3, pin 4 is toggled and pin 5 is lowered. On the falling edge of pin 3, pin 5 is raised. Note that we can refer to the flag register and bit either by directly using the VPORTF.INTFLAGS or by the pins.h defined intflg.digital_3.

```
ISR(PORTF_PORT_vect) {
  if (VPORTF.INTFLAGS & ( 1 << 5)) { // or intflg.digital_3
    if (pin.digital_3 != 0) {
      pin.digital_4 = 1; // toggle pin 4
      port.digital_5 = 0; // lower pin 5
    } else {
      port.digital_5 = 1; // raise pin 5
    }
    //  VPORTF.INTFLAGS |= (1 << 5); // clear the flag or
    intflg.digital_3 = 1; // this way is the same
  }
}
```

The oscilloscope showing pins 3, 4, and 5 from top to bottom.

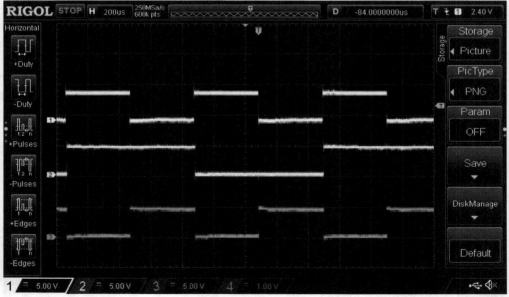

This short program can be easily modified to try out other interrupt modes and actions on the pins.

Events

The Event system can generate events from GPIO pins and GPIO pins can also be event users. The preceding example program has additional lines in the setup function to demonstrate events:

```
EVSYS.CHANNEL0 = EVSYS_GENERATOR_TCB1_CMP0_gc;
EVSYS.USEREVOUTA = EVSYS_CHANNEL_CHANNEL0_gc;
EVSYS.CHANNEL4 = EVSYS_GENERATOR_PORT1_PIN5_gc;
EVSYS.USEREVOUTD = EVSYS_CHANNEL_CHANNEL4_gc;
```

Channel 0 is driven by Timer/Counter B channel 0, which is the one creating the PWM signal on Arduino pin 3. That event is connected to USEREVOUTA, which is pin A4. Channel 4 is driven by Arduino pin 3. That event is connected to USEREVOUTD, which is pin A1. Using the oscilloscope we can view pins 3, A1, and A4, from top to bottom:

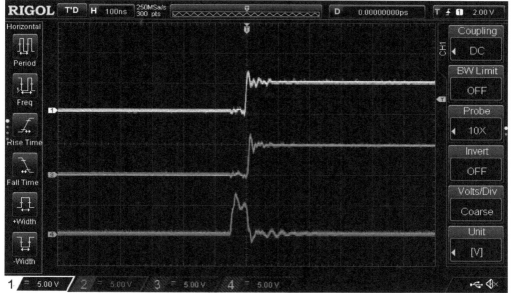

Note that the pulse from TCB1_CMP0 is only 50ns (one clock period) wide. The delay from pin 3 to A1 is 6ns.

Port Multiplexer and Peripheral Override

The Port Multiplexer determines which port pins are connected to the various peripherals. Since the default values of the multiplexer are not used in the Arduino Nano Every, it is important to consult the Rosetta Stone table to determine the exact pin assignments.

In almost every case, enabling the associated peripheral overrides the GPIO functionality for the pins, which means that if the pin is being used as an output for a peripheral it is unnecessary to change the pin direction to output. Any exceptions are documented in the peripheral description. The GPIO interface can read the value on the pin, even if it is being used by a peripheral.

Using the AREF and RESET pins as GPIO pins

Unlike the Arduino Nano board, the Nano Every AREF and RESET pins can be used as GPIO pins. However there are some limitations imposed by the board.

The AREF pin is normally used for an external analog reference voltage, but it is a normal GPIO pin, Port D bit 7. There is $4.8\mu F$ of capacitance on this pin which will slow it down as a digital pin, but it still would be useful for driving an LED, for instance. The Pins.h library gives this the name *aref_pin*.

The RESET pin normally resets the microcontroller when grounded. This functionality was needed to start the bootloader on the ATmega328P based Arduino boards, but is not necessary with the ATmega4809. A fuse bit disables the reset function, so to use this pin as a GPIO pin requires changing a line in the boards.txt file. Find the line:

```
nona4809.bootloader.SYSCFG0=0xC9
```
and change it to:
```
nona4809.bootloader.SYSCFG0=0xC1
```

The RESET pin is connected to the an external pullup resistor, a small bypass capacitor, and the reset pushbutton to ground. While the pin could be used as an output pin, one would have to be careful not to press the reset button as that would short the output driver circuit. The best use is as an input pin, possibly using that reset button as an input. The Pins.h library gives this pin the name *reset_pin*.

CHAPTER TWELVE

Analog to Digital Converter

The analog to digital converter in the ATmega4809 is similar to that of the ATmega328p but for 8 times greater speed, additional reference voltages, the ability to make multiple samples for a single conversion, and window comparisons. The time between samples can be randomized to achieve immunity from harmonics. But the basic operation is the same, and the examples from *Far Inside The Arduino* will be repeated here, modified for the ATmega4809. The ATmega4809 versions can be downloaded from the website.

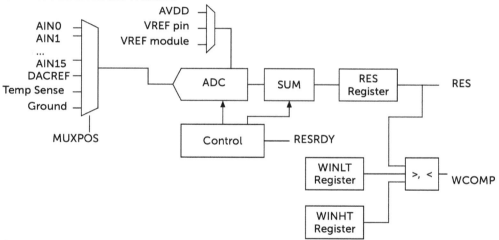

The digital input circuitry should be disabled on any pins used for analog signals. This is done setting the pin's PORTx.PINnCTRL register to PORT_ISC_INPUT_DISABLE_gc.

Control A Register ADC0.CTRLA

Bit	7	6	5	4	3	2	1	0
Function	RUNSTBY					RESSEL	FREERUN	ENABLE

RUNSTBY allows running in Standby Sleep mode. RESSEL is resolution selection; normally resolution is 10 bits but set this bit for truncating the result to 8 bits. FREERUN enables free-running mode where a new conversion starts immediately after the current conversion ends. The ENABLE bit turns on the converter.

Control B Register ADC0.CTRLB

The converter will accumulate multiple sample results, sum them and then indicate conversion complete. More samples will reduce the noise in measurements but take more time and effectively reduces the frequency response. Values allowed are 0 through 6, corresponding to 2^n results (1 to 64).

Control C Register ADC0.CTRLC

Bit	7	6	5	4	3	2	1	0
Function		SAMPCAP	REFSEL			PRESC		

SAMPCAP selects the sample capacitance in the sample and hold circuit at the front end of the converter. A value of 0, corresponding to 10pf, is recommended for reference voltages of less than 1V and a value of 1, corresponding to 5pf, is recommended for higher reference voltages.

REFSEL selects the voltage reference. Voltages can be measured between 0 and the reference voltage. A value of 0, ADC_REFSEL_INTREF_gc, uses the internal reference from the VREF module. A value of 1, ADC_REFSEL_VDDREF_gc, uses VDD. A value of 2, ADC_REFSEL_VREFA_gc, uses the external VREF pin, which is labeled AREF on the Arduino Nano Every board. This pin would need to be connected to a voltage reference between 0 and VDD. Note that unlike in the ATmega328P part, the AREF pin is not an output pin for internal voltage references.

The internal reference is set in a field of VREF.CTRLA. This register is shared with the reference setting for the analog comparator. VREF takes $25\mu s$ to stabilize. Values are:

Value	Constant	Voltage
0	VREF_ADC0REFSEL_0V55_gc	0.55 volts
1	VREF_ADC0REFSEL_1V1_gc	1.1 volts
2	VREF_ADC0REFSEL_2V5_gc	2.5 volts
3	VREF_ADC0REFSEL_4V34_gc	4.34 volts
4	VREF_ADC0REFSEL_1V5_gc	1.5 volts

PRESC sets the division factor from the system clock to the ADC clock. The ADC clock should be no faster than 1.5MHz for maximum resolution. So for a 20MHz clock, that would be a division by 14 and for a 16MHz clock that would be a division by 11. Division factors are powers of two (1 / $2^{(PRESC+1)}$) so /16 must be used, which is PRESC=3. This gives a 1MHz ADC clock, $1\mu s$, for 16MHz system clock and a 1.25MHz ADC clock, $0.8\mu s$, for the 20MHz system clock. The conversion time is 13 ADC clock periods plus any additional periods from the settings of INITDLY, SAMPDLY, and SAMPLEN.

However if the 0.55 volt reference is used, the ADC clock frequency should be reduced below 260kHz. This would call for a setting of 5 with a 16MHz clock or 6 with a 20MHz clock. Running faster than these recommended values requires special considerations discussed in the ATmega4809 data sheet.

Control D Register ADC0.CTRLD

Bit	7	6	5	4	3	2	1	0
Function	INITDLY			ASDV	SAMPDLY			

INITDLY sets an initial startup delay. The documentation does not specify how much delay is needed for the converter other than suggesting a delay greater than $32\mu s$. Values of 0 through 5 give delays of 0, 16, 32, 64, 128, or 246 ADC clock cycles. ASDV enables the automatic sampling delay variation. The delay between samples, set in the SAMPDLY field, can vary between 0 and 15 ADC clock cycles. When ASDV is on the SAMPDLY field is incremented by one (wrapping from 15 to 0) with each sample.

Control E Register ADC0.CTRLE
The lower three bits set the Window Comparator Mode. The window comparator uses 16 bit registers ADC0.RESULT, ADC0.WINLT, and ADC0.WINHT to create a windowing function that can trigger the ADC0_WCOMP interrupt. Values are:

Value	Constant	Triggers on
0	ADC_WINCM_NONE_gc	(disabled)
1	ADC_WINCM_BELOW_gc	RESULT < WINLT
2	ADC_WINCM_ABOVE_gc	RESULT > WINHT
3	ADC_WINCM_INSIDE_gc	WINLT < RESULT < WINHT
4	ADC_WINCM_OUTSIDE_gc	RESULT < WINLT or RESULT > WINHT

MUXPOS Register ADC0.MUXPOS
Selects the analog input for the next conversion. If value is changed during a conversion, the value won't take effect until the conversion completes. The values do not linearly correspond to the pin numbers, so set carefully!

Value	Constant	Input, Arduino Nano Every
0	ADC_MUXPOS_AIN0_gc	PD0, Pin A3
1	ADC_MUXPOS_AIN1_gc	PD1, Pin A2
2	ADC_MUXPOS_AIN2_gc	PD2, Pin A1
3	ADC_MUXPOS_AIN3_gc	PD3, Pin A0
4	ADC_MUXPOS_AIN4_gc	PD4, Pin A6
5	ADC_MUXPOS_AIN5_gc	PD5, Pin A7
6	ADC_MUXPOS_AIN6_gc	Not accessible
7	ADC_MUXPOS_AIN7_gc	PD7, AREF
8	ADC_MUXPOS_AIN8_gc	PE0, Pin 11
9	ADC_MUXPOS_AIN9_gc	PE1, Pin 12
0x0A	ADC_MUXPOS_AIN10_gc	PE2, Pin 13
0x0B	ADC_MUXPOS_AIN11_gc	PE3, Pin 8
0x0C	ADC_MUXPOS_AIN12_gc	PF2, Pin A4 *
0x0D	ADC_MUXPOS_AIN13_gc	PF3, Pin A5 *
0xoE	ADC_MUXPOS_AIN14_gc	PF4, Pin 6
0x0F	ADC_MUXPOS_AIN15_gc	PF5, Pin 3
0x1C	ADC_MUXPOS_DACREF_gc	Analog Comparator DAC
0x1E	ADC_MUXPOS_TEMPSENSE_gc	Temperature Sensor
0x1F	ADC_MUXPOS_GND_gc	Ground

* Note that ports PF2 is connected to PA2, and PF3 is connected to PA3, so when using these inputs the digital input of the port A pin(s) should be disabled as well as those of the port F pin(s).

The selection of DACREF uses the output of the DAC in the Analog Comparator. Using the temperature sensor needs to follow the instructions in the ATmega4809 data sheet. Example code can be found in the first example program in this section.

Sample Control Register ADC0.SAMPCTRL
This 5 bit field lengthens the sampling time by this number of ADC clock cycles, 0 to 31. This will provide more accurate results with high impedance sources.

Command and Event Control Registers ADC0.COMMAND and ADC0.EVCTRL

Writing a "1" to ADC0.COMMAND will start a single measurement or start continuous conversion if enabled. When read, this bit indicates that a conversion is in progress.

The Event System can also be used to start a conversion. To enable event user EVSYS.USERADC0 for this, the least significant bit in ADC0.EVCTRL must be set to "1".

Interrupt Control and Flags Registers ADC0.INTCTRL and ADC0.INTFLAGS

Bit	7	6	5	4	3	2	1	0
Function							WCOMP	RESRDY

The interrupt enable bits are in INTCTRL and the interrupt flags in INTFLAGS.

The RESRDY flag indicates that a measurement is complete and the result can be read in the ADC0.RES register. Reading the RES register or writing a "1" to the RESRDY flag will clear the flag. If the RESRDY interrupt is enabled, the ADC0_RESRDY interrupt will be requested.

The WCOMP flag indicates that a measurement is complete the windowing trigger conditions have been met. Reading the RES register or writing a "1" to the WCOMP flag will clear the flag. If the WCOMP interrupt is enabled, the ADC0_WCOMP interrupt will be requested.

Result ADC0.RES 16-bit register

The result of the conversion, which may consist of multiple samples added together, is available from this register. Circuitry in the microcontroller insures that the 16-bit read will be atomic even if an interrupt occurs between reading each byte.

Windows Comparator Low and High Thresholds ADC0.WINLT and ADC0.WINHT 16-bit registers

These registers hold the threshold values for the windowing function. If there are multiple samples in a measurement then the values must be scaled up accordingly as the comparisons are made to the RES register and not to individual samples.

Example Programs

Example Program adc_1

The first example program measures the voltage on pin A2 then measures the internal temperature. Pin A2 can be connected to the 3.3v pin to provide a voltage to measure. Interrupts are not used and the example functions much like using the *analogRead* function.

The setup function disables digital input on pin A2 and enables the ADC module:

```
PORTD.PIN1CTRL = PORT_ISC_INPUT_DISABLE_gc; // Disable digital on A2
(Pin PD1)
ADC0.CTRLA = 1; // Enable the ADC
```

Functions are used to perform the measurements. Each function does all necessary configuration for the specific measurement. To measure A2 we have:

```
int getA2(void) {
  ADC0.CTRLC = ADC_SAMPCAP_bm + 1 * (1 << ADC_REFSEL_gp) + 3;
                    // VDD reference, correct clock divisor (16)
  ADC0.MUXPOS = ADC_MUXPOS_AIN1_gc; // This is input from pin A2
  ADC0.CTRLD = 0; // Turn off all delays
                 // (used in the temperature measurements)
  ADC0.SAMPCTRL = 0;
  ADC0.COMMAND = 1; // Start the conversion
  // wait for completion
  while ((ADC0.INTFLAGS & ADC_RESRDY_bm) == 0) ;
  return (ADC0.RES * 5000L) / 1024; // Return voltage in millivolts
}
```

Getting the temperature reading is more involved and uses the Voltage Reference module.

```
int getTemperature(void) {
  VREF.CTRLA = VREF_ADC0REFSEL_1V1_gc; // 1.1 volt reference
  ADC0.CTRLC = ADC_SAMPCAP_bm + 3;
                 // VREF reference, correct clock divisor
  ADC0.MUXPOS = ADC_MUXPOS_TEMPSENSE_gc; // Select temperature sensor
  ADC0.CTRLD = 2 * (1 << ADC_INITDLY_gp); // Initial delay of 32us
  ADC0.SAMPCTRL = 31; // Maximum length sample time (32us is desired)
  ADC0.COMMAND = 1; // Start the conversion
  while ((ADC0.INTFLAGS & ADC_RESRDY_bm) == 0) ;
                      // wait for completion
  // The following code is based on the ATmega4809 data sheet
  int8_t sigrow_offset = SIGROW.TEMPSENSE1;
                      // Read signed value from signature row
  uint8_t sigrow_gain = SIGROW.TEMPSENSE0;
                      // Read unsigned value from signature row
  uint16_t adc_reading = ADC0.RES;
              // ADC conversion result with 1.1 V internal reference
  uint32_t temp = adc_reading - sigrow_offset;
  temp *= sigrow_gain; // Result might overflow (10bit+8bit)
  temp += 0x80; // Add 1/2 to get correct rounding on division below
  temp >>= 8; // Divide result to get Kelvin
  uint16_t temperature_in_K = temp;
  return temperature_in_K - 273; // Return Celsius temperature
}
```

Example Program *adc_2*

This program uses free running mode. The value in ADC0.RES is always the most recent conversion result. To make things more interesting, we will take 8 samples for each measurement. This means the total measurement time will be 104μs (83.2μs with 20MHz clock). We will display the most recent conversion result ten times a second. We will also use the internal 4.34 volt reference so the measurement will be more accurate. This will, of course, limit the maximum voltage to 4.34 volts. If you measure the 3.3 volt source you will probably find the measured value to be more accurate than in example program adc_1.

In free running mode, we do the configuration in the setup function and read the result any time we want.

```
void setup() {
  Serial.begin(9600);
  VREF.CTRLA = VREF_ADC0REFSEL_4V34_gc; // 4.34 volt reference
  PORTD.PIN1CTRL = PORT_ISC_INPUT_DISABLE_gc; // Disable digital on A2
(Pin PD1)
  ADC0.CTRLA = ADC_FREERUN_bm + ADC_ENABLE_bm; // Enable the ADC in
free run mode
  ADC0.CTRLB = 3; // 8 samples per measurement (2^3)
  ADC0.CTRLC = ADC_SAMPCAP_bm + 3; // VDD reference, correct clock
divisor (16)
  ADC0.MUXPOS = ADC_MUXPOS_AIN1_gc; // This is input from pin A2
  ADC0.COMMAND = 1; // Start the conversion
  delay(700);
}
```

To print the voltage in millivolts:

```
  // Scaling takes into account 4.34 volt reference and the 8 samples
  Serial.println(ADC0.RES * 4340L / (1024 * 8));
```

Example Program *adc_3*

This program reads the voltages on A0 through A5 sequentially. An interrupt routine is used to save the values in an array and start the conversion on the next input. Except for indexing the analog input pins and result array, and the use of the RESRDY interrupt, there are no new concepts here. Read the example program for details.

Example Program *adc_3_smoothed*

This program is a modification of *adc_3* that applies either a software low-pass filter or uses multiple (16) samples to smooth the results. Define LOW_PASS_FILTER for the low-pass filter version. You can use this program to compare the two techniques. You might also want to turn on ASDV when taking multiple samples.

CHAPTER THIRTEEN

Analog Comparator

The analog comparator compares the voltages on two pins, or one pin against an internal DAC. The output of the comparator can be used as an event source, be read as a status bit, or trigger an interrupt based on changing comparison state.

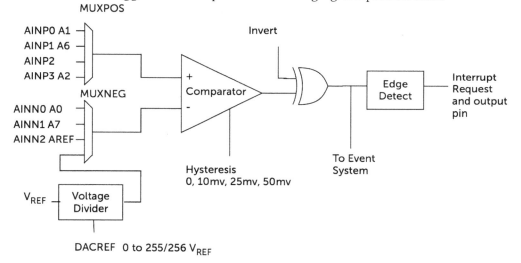

The digital input circuitry should be disabled on any pins used for analog signals. This is done setting the pin's PORTx.PINnCTRL register to PORT_ISC_INPUT_DISABLE_gc.

There are five associated registers.

Control A Register AC0.CTRLA

Bit	7	6	5	4	3	2	1	0
Function	RUNSTBY	OUTEN	INTMODE		LPMODE		HYSMODE	ENABLE

This is the primary configuration register. RUNSTBY enables operation in sleep mode. OUTEN enables the output pin, which is not accessible on the Arduino Nano Every board. INTMODE has a value 0 to interrupt on both edges, 2 to interrupt when the comparator output goes low, or 3 to interrupt when the comparator output goes high. LPMODE halves the power consumption but slows the response time. HYSMODE adjusts the hysteresis from 0v (value 0), 10mv (1), 25mv(2), to 50mv (3). Hysteresis should be turned on to have noise immunity. Finally the ENABLE bit enables the comparator.

Even though the output pin is not accessible on the Arduino Nano Every board, the output of the comparator can still be output using the Event System. For instance, the following will bring the comparator output to pin 5 on the board:

```
EVSYS.CHANNEL0 = EVSYS_GENERATOR_AC0_OUT_gc; // Connect AC to pin 5
EVSYS.USEREVOUTB = EVSYS_CHANNEL_CHANNEL0_gc;
```

Mux Control Register AC0.MUXCTRLA

Bit	7	6	5	4	3	2	1	0
Function	INVERT			MUXPOS			MUXNEG	

This configuration register is used to select the inputs to the comparator. Additionally, the INVERT bit inverts the comparator output. Normally the output is high if the voltage on the positive input is greater than the voltage on the negative input. The choices for the positive input are:

Value	Name, Port	Board Location
0	AINP0, PD2	Pin A1
1	AINP1, PD4	Pin A6
2	AINP2, PD6	Not accessible
3	AINP3, PD1	Pin A2

The choices for the negative input are:

Value	Name	Board Location
0	AINN0, PD3	Pin A0
1	AINN1, PD5	Pin A7
2	AINN2, PD7	AREF
3	DACREF	Not applicable

Of particular interest is the DACREF choice, which allows comparing the positive input with an adjustable voltage of a built-in DAC. The register AC0.DACREF sets the DAC voltage, and is VREF*DACREF/256. The reference voltage VREF comes from the Voltage Reference module, and can be set to several fixed, accurate voltages or to AVDD, analog VDD, which is nominally 5.0 volts. One register in VREF sets the reference voltages for both the ADC and Analog Comparator. The default value is to use a 0.55V reference, but most useful is either the 4.34 volt reference:

```
VREF.CTRLA = VREF_AC0REFSEL_4V34_gc;
```

or AVDD:

```
VREF.CTRLA = VREF_AC0REFSEL_AVDD_gc
```

Analog comparator interrupts are enabled with a "1" in the least significant bit of the AC0.INTCTRL register. In the interrupt service routine, the interrupt flag, the least significant bit in the AC0.STATUS register must be cleared (it isn't cleared automatically) by writing a "1" to it.

The comparator example program is provided as *comparator_test*. It uses a filtered PWM output with a sweeping duty cycle to create a trapezoidal waveform. The analog comparator compares the waveform voltage with a 2.5 volt reference as set by AC0.DACREF and the VREF voltage set to AVDD. The event system is used to connect the comparator output to pin 5. Additionally the module is configured to interrupt on both edges of the comparator output. The interrupt service routine toggles pin 2 while the waveform generator clears pin 2 at the minimum and maximum points. If the hysteresis is sufficient to avoid noise then pin 2 will go high at each comparison match. If the hysteresis is insufficient, the noise will cause multiple matches and interrupts at each crossing. Also, because the waveform is so slow, low power mode is enabled.

This code in the setup function configures the event system channel, the voltage reference, and the comparator:

```
PORTD.PIN2CTRL = PORT_ISC_INPUT_DISABLE_gc; // Disable digital on A1
EVSYS.CHANNEL0 = EVSYS_GENERATOR_AC0_OUT_gc; // Connect AC to pin 5
EVSYS.USEREVOUTB = EVSYS_CHANNEL_CHANNEL0_gc;
VREF.CTRLA = VREF_AC0REFSEL_AVDD_gc; // Set ref for AC DAC to VDD
AC0.MUXCTRLA = 3; // A1 is positive, DAC is negative
AC0.DACREF = 128; // Mid scale, 2.5 volts
AC0.CTRLA = 0x0f; // Enable comparator with 50mv hysteresis,
                  // interrupt on both edges, low power
AC0.INTCTRL = 1; // Enable AC interrupt
```

The interrupt service routine is straightforward:

```
ISR(AC0_AC_vect) {
  pin.digital_2 = 1; // toggle on match -- should always be
                     // 0 -> 1 if sufficient hysteresis
  AC0.STATUS = 1; // Reset interrupt flag
}
```

Here's the oscilloscope capture of operation:

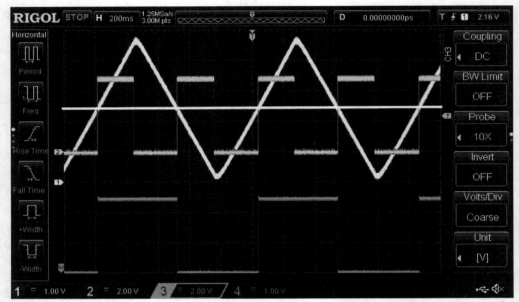

The white line was added to show the 2.5 volt level of the trapezoid waveform. The upper square wave is the voltage on pin 2, while the lower square wave is the comparator output viewed via the event system.

CHAPTER FOURTEEN

Timer "A"

The ATMega4809 has five 16-bit Timer/Counters, one type *A* and four type *B*. These have different designs and will be covered separately. This section is about Timer/Counter A. It consists of a base counter with control logic and three compare channels. This Timer/Counter can also be split into two separate 8-bit counters each with three compare channels.

The Arduino library uses Timer/Counter A to provide the *analogWrite* function (PWM) on digital pins 9, 10, and 5 respectively for the three compare channels 0, 1, and 2. It treats the Timer/Counter as though it is 8-bit. With the pin assignments made, while split mode would give 6 PWM pins, the additional three pins are not brought out on the Arduino Every board. So we will only consider 16-bit operation and not look at split mode.

The Timer/Counter A can be used for three PWM outputs with the same period and resolution. Or it can be used as a frequency generator with three different phases. It can be used for periodic interrupts. And finally it has a counter mode counting events or gated by events. The event input comes from the Event System. The Timer/Counter can also generate events for the Event System.

Base Counter

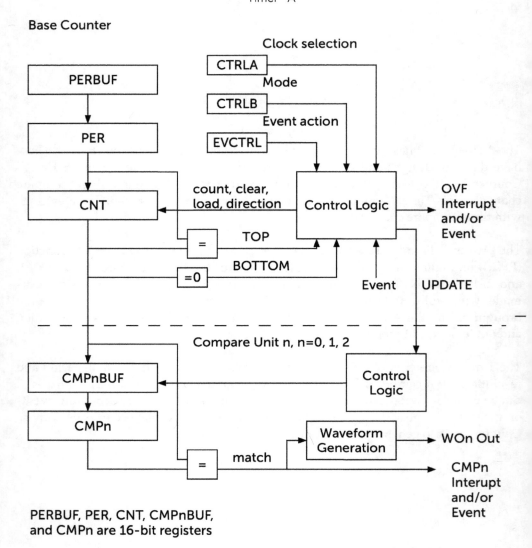

PERBUF, PER, CNT, CMPnBUF,
and CMPn are 16-bit registers

There are three data registers in the base counter, PERBUF, PER, and CNT. Each compare unit has two data registers, CMPnBUF and CMPn, for n=0, 1 or 2. The BUF registers are buffers. These registers can be written at any time and their contents (if they are written to) are transferred at a time when it won't affect the current operation cycle. A major addition compared to the ATmega328P is that there is a new PER (period) register that can control the period of the base counter. The registers are:

Control A Register TCA0.SINGLE.CTRLA

Bit	7	6	5	4	3	2	1	0
Function					CLKSEL			ENABLE

The ENABLE bit enables the timer/counter. The CLKSEL bits set the clock divider that sets the timer/counter clock speed as a fraction of the system clock speed. The Arduino library sets the speed to /64 so the CNT register counts at a 250kHz rate with a 16MHz clock. When the 20MHz clock is used the CNT register will count at 312.5kHz. The Arduino library uses the TCA0 clock divider for the TCB timer/counters, so changing this value will effect the time tracking functions *millis*, *micros*, and *delay*, as well as any functions that use these like *pulseInLong*. See the discussion in discussion of Timer "B". Choices are:

Value	Constant name	Description
0	TCA_SINGLE_CLKSEL_DIV1_gc	/1
1	TCA_SINGLE_CLKSEL_DIV2_gc	/2
2	TCA_SINGLE_CLKSEL_DIV4_gc	/4
3	TCA_SINGLE_CLKSEL_DIV8_gc	/8
4	TCA_SINGLE_CLKSEL_DIV16_gc	/16
5	TCA_SINGLE_CLKSEL_DIV64_gc	/64
6	TCA_SINGLE_CLKSEL_DIV256_gc	/256
7	TCA_SINGLE_CLKSEL_DIV1024_gc	/1024

Control B Register TCA0.SINGLE.CTRLB

Bit	7	6	5	4	3	2	1	0
Function		CMP2EN	CMP1EN	CMP0EN	ALUPD	WGMODE		

When in the FRQ or PWM waveform modes, the CMPnEN bits enable the WOn outputs. Note that the direction of the pin must be set to output. In NORMAL generation mode, these bits are inactive. The ALUPD bit is for Auto-Lock Update. If 1, LUPD (in CTRLE) is set to 1 until all enabled compare channel buffers are valid, then the LUPD bit is cleared. In most applications synchronizing the updates is not a concern.

The WGMODE bits set the waveform generation mode. The choices are:
- *Normal Mode (value 0, TCA_SINGLE_WGMODE_NORMAL_gc)* — in this mode no waveforms are generated. CNT counts from 0 through PER (PER+1 timer clock periods) and resets. At the top value OVF is indicated and any

UPDATE from buffer registers occurs. The CNT register can also count down in this mode, but that is not the normal mode of operation.

- *Frequency (FRQ) (value 1, TCA_SINGLE_WGMODE_FRQ_gc)* — This mode uses CMP0 and not PER to reset the counter. When the counter resets the output WO0 toggles. The frequency is (counter frequency)/2(CMP0+1). At the top value of CNT OVF is indicated and any UPDATE from buffer registers occurs. Comparison CMP1 and CMP2 as well as outputs WO1 and WO2 are not used.

- *Single Slope PWM (value 3, TCA_SINGLE_WGMODE_SINGLESLOPE_gc)* — In this mode CNT counts from 0 to PER like in Normal mode, and the frequency of the PWM signal is (counter frequency)/(PER+1). The CMPn register adjusts the duty cycle for each of the three outputs independently. A value of 0 will produce a low output while that greater than PER will produce a high output. The duty cycle is CMPn/(PER+1). At the CNT value of 0 OVF is indicated and any UPDATE from the buffer registers occurs.

- *Dual Slope PWM* (value 5, 6, or 7, TCA_SINGLE_WGMODE_DSTOP_gc, DSBOTH or DSBOTTOM) — In these modes CNT counts up to PER then reverses and counts down to 0. The frequency is (counter frequency)/2PER and the duty cycle is CMPn/PER. UPDATE occurs when the CNT is 0. OVF is indicated when CNT=PER in TOP mode, CNT=0 in BOTTOM mode, or CNT=PER or 0 in BOTH mode. Using dual slope PWM rather than single slope PWM eliminates the phase shift that occurs when changing the duty cycle.

Note that the INVERT bit of the port pin's PINnCTRL register can be used to invert the PWM signal.

The Arduino library uses Single Slope PWM, PER=255, and a /64 divisor. This gives a period of 1.024ms, a frequency of 977Hz. CMPn values of 0 through 256 give 0 through 100% duty cycle. The *analogWrite* function has a range of 0 through 256 for the Arduino Nano Every board and not the range 0 through 255 when used with other AVR boards.

Control C, D, E, F Registers

These registers have limited usefulness. CTRLC allows setting or clearing the output pins when the timer/counter is not running, but this can be done by disabling the output (CMPnEN) and writing to the PORT.OUT register directly. CTRLD enables split mode, not discussed here and not useful with the Arduino board. CTRLE comes only in SET and CLR versions and allows overriding normal operation. CTRLF also comes only in SET and CLR versions and allows reading, setting, or clearing the buffer valid bits.

Event Control Register TCA0.SINGLE.EVCTRL

Bit	7	6	5	4	3	2	1	0
Function					EVACT			CNTEI

Instead of CNT being incremented from the clock, it can be controlled from an event via the USERTCA0 event user. CNTEI=1 enables this mode while EVACT selects the method CNT will count. A possible design error (at least it isn't documented) interferes with the TCA clock prescaler from being used for Timer/Counter B when CNTE1=1. This may preclude the use of the event counting mode since the Arduino library uses the TCA prescaler source on all TCB channels. However see the last example program in this chapter.

Value	Constant name	Description
0	TCA_SINGLE_EVACT_POSEDGE_gc	Count on positive event edge
1	TCA_SINGLE_EVACT_ANYEDGE_gc	Count on both event edges
2	TCA_SINGLE_EVACT_HIGHLVL_gc	Count timer/counter clock cycles when event signal is high
3	TCA_SINGLE_EVACT_UPDOWN_gc	Count timer/counter clock cycles. Count up when event signal is low and count down when it is high

The HIGHLVL mode could be useful for measuring pulse widths. If a 16 bit counter is not big enough, the OVL interrupt can be used to increment a counter extension. In general, the type B Timer/Counter is easier to use for event capture functions and won't require disabling the TCA prescaler.

The Timer/Counter can also generate events:
TCA Overflow (EVSYS_GENERATOR_TCA0_OVF_LUNF_gc)
TCA Compare match channel n (EVSYS_GENERATOR_TCA0_CMPn_gc) n=0,1,2

Interrupt Control and Flag Registers TCA0.SINGLE.INTCTRL and TCA.SINGLE.INTFLAGS

Bit	7	6	5	4	3	2	1	0
Function		CMP2	CMP1	CMP0				OVF

In the interrupt control register, CMPn enables interrupts for CMPn matching CNT. OVF enables the interrupt for CNT register OVF (register has reached maximum value or minimum, 0, value depending on the WGMODE). The interrupt vectors are TCA0_CMP0, TCA0_CMP1, TCA0_CMP2, and TCA0_OVF.

In the interrupt flag register, the bits must be cleared by writing a "1" to the bit.

Period, Counter, Compare n registers TCA0.SINGLE.PER, TCA0.SINGLE.CNT, TCA0.SINGLE.CMPn, n=0 through 2
These are 16-bit registers.

Period Buffer, Compare Buffer registers, TCA0.SINGLE.PERBUF, TCA0.SINGLE.CMPnBUF, n=0 through 2
Writing to one of these 16-bit registers sets the buffer valid bit for the register. When the UPDATE state occurs, if the buffer valid bit is set then the value gets transferred to the normal period or compare register and then the buffer valid bit is cleared. This insures the normal register only gets updated at a safe time that won't create an irregular output.

Example Programs

There are five example programs, one for each of four waveform generation modes, and one using the Event System to measure a pulse width. The first example program *TCA_NORMAL* uses Normal mode. This can be used to generate a periodic interrupt, however we can do that in any mode with the advantage of performing other functions simultaneously. Configuration is straightforward:

```
TCA0.SINGLE.PERBUF = 24; // Sets OVF period to 25 * 4us, 100us
                         // Will give a 5kHz frequency square wave
TCA0.SINGLE.INTCTRL = 0x1; // OVF
TCA0.SINGLE.CTRLB = 0x0; // Enable NORMAL mode
```

And in the example, the overflow interrupt simply toggles a pin:

```
ISR(TCA0_OVF_vect) {
  pin.digital_2 = 1; // toggle pin
  TCA0.SINGLE.INTFLAGS = 1; // reset flag
}
```

The second program, *TCA_FRQ*, uses Frequency mode. Three pins output the waveform, overflow, and compare.

```
ddr.digital_9 = 1; // WO0
ddr.digital_10 = 1; // CMP0 toggles this
ddr.digital_2 = 1; // OVF toggles this
TCA0.SINGLE.CMP0BUF = 24; // Sets square wave period to (24 + 1)*2
// Timer/Counter clocks, 5 kHz
TCA0.SINGLE.INTCTRL = 0x11; // OVF and CMP0 interrupts
TCA0.SINGLE.CTRLB = 0x11; // Enable CMP0 and FRQ mode
```

There is one added interrupt service routine for the CMP0 interrupt:

```
ISR(TCA0_CMP0_vect) {
  pin.digital_10 = 1;
  TCA0.SINGLE.INTFLAGS = 0x10; // reset flag
```

}

All three pins change at roughly the same time, but, of course, W00, changes first since there is no interrupt latency, and the OVF interrupt pin changes before the CMP0 interrupt pin because it is higher priority:

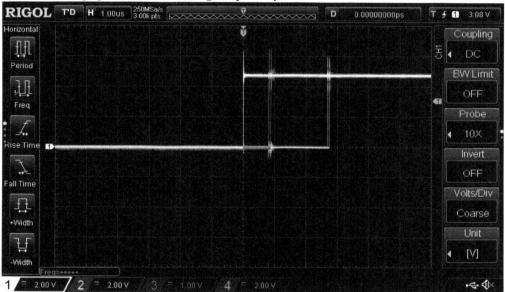

In common operation in the Arduino, the waveform mode is single slope, as demonstrated in example program *TCA_PWM3*. Three pins provide three separate PWM outputs, here set to 25%, 50%, and 75% duty cycle. A fourth pin is toggled by the OVF interrupt. The Arduino library does not use this interrupt, but it is suitable for a periodic interrupt for such things as running state machines or debouncing keyboards. Configuration is:

```
ddr.digital_9 = 1; // WO0
ddr.digital_10 = 1; // WO1
ddr.digital_5 = 1; // WO2
ddr.digital_2 = 1; // OVF toggles this
TCA0.SINGLE.PERBUF = 255; // 1.024ms period
TCA0.SINGLE.CMP0BUF = 64; // 25% duty cycle
TCA0.SINGLE.CMP1BUF = 128; // 50% duty cycle
TCA0.SINGLE.CMP2BUF = 192; // 75% duty cycle
TCA0.SINGLE.INTCTRL = 1; // OVF
TCA0.SINGLE.CTRLB = 0x73; // Three channels on, Single Slope PWM
```

The oscilloscope display shows that the leading edge of any output is at the same point in time which means the center of the pulse moves, changing the phase.

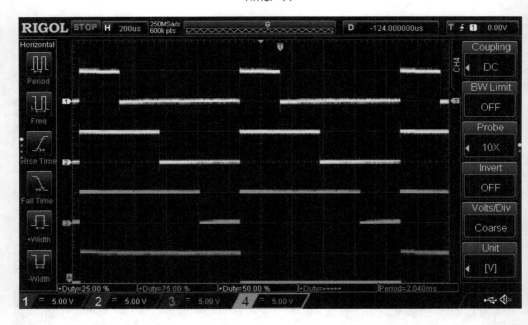

Dual slope PWM is used in the example program *TCA_DSPWM3*. Initialization differs in only two lines:

```
TCA0.SINGLE.PERBUF = 256; // Period is 2.048ms
...
TCA0.SINGLE.CTRLB = 0x76; // Three channels on, Dual Slope PWM
```

OVF interrupt will occur at both the minimum and maximum CNT values with the choice made, keeping the same interrupt rate as with the single slope PWM.

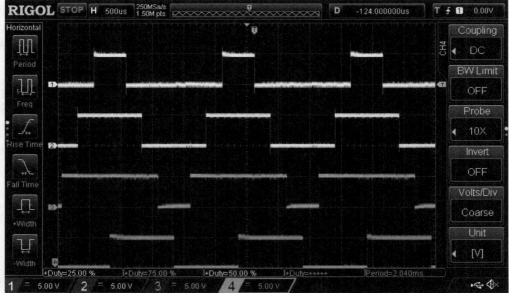

The final example program, *TCA_PW*, uses the Event System to measure a pulse width. As mentioned earlier, this precludes the use of the TCA prescaler for the four Timer/Counter B. In order to run this example program the System Time Tracking function of TCB3 must be changed to not use the TCA prescaler. This change is part of the modifications given in the chapter Chapter Sixteen - A Better Timer Setup (page 67).

A pulse train of 8μs wide pulses is generated using the PWM on board pin 3, which is port PF5. This pin is from TCB1, which must be modified to use the system clock rather than the prescaler of TCA. The Event System routes PF5 to TCA0 event input. TCA is configured to count while the event input is high. The TCA prescaler is set to /1 to get the greatest precision of measurement. PF5 is set to cause a port pin interrupt when it goes low so the program can capture the pulse width.

Configuration is:
```
analogWrite(3, 64); // 8 us high 24 us low
TCB1.CTRLA = 3; // 0.125 us rate
EVSYS.CHANNEL4 = EVSYS_GENERATOR_PORT1_PIN5_gc; // Route pin 3, PF5
EVSYS.USERTCA0 = EVSYS_CHANNEL_CHANNEL4_gc; // to TCA0
TCA0.SINGLE.CTRLA = TCA_SINGLE_CLKSEL_DIV1_gc | 1;
                        // Run TCA at 16MHz.
TCA0.SINGLE.PERBUF = 0xffff; // Allow maximum count
TCA0.SINGLE.CTRLB = TCA_SINGLE_WGMODE_NORMAL_gc; // Normal mode.
TCA0.SINGLE.EVCTRL = TCA_SINGLE_EVACT_HIGHLVL_gc | 1;
                        // Count while high
PORTF.PIN5CTRL = PORT_ISC_FALLING_gc; // Interrupt on pin 3 falling.
```

The ISR is:
```
ISR(PORTF_PORT_vect) {
  width = TCA0.SINGLE.CNT; // Get time high in counter ticks
  TCA0.SINGLE.CNT = 0; // And reset count
  intflg.digital_3 = 1; // clear interrupt flag
}
```

CHAPTER FIFTEEN

Timer "B"

Timer/Counter "B" consists of four independent 16-bit timer/counters. B0 and B1 are used for PWM (*analogWrite*) on pins 6 and 3, respectively. B1 is also used by the library *tone* function and B3 is used for the time tracking functions *millis, micros, delay,* and functions that use them like *pulseInLong*. When the *tone* function is being used, PWM on pin 3 is not available. The Arduino library uses B2 for the Servo library. The outputs of B2 and B3 are not brought out to pins on the Arduino board, but can be used as event generators (port pin input or CAPT interrupt flag set pulse).

There are a few complicating factors in using the Timer/Counters in the presence of the Arduino library. The first problem is that the clock divider of Timer/Counter A is the only divider available (other than a divide by two) for any of the Timer/Counter B. This means that if the divider is changed to benefit PWM generation in Timer/Counter A (faster rates to increase performance, for instance) then the time functions won't work properly and in fact increased interrupt rates could "hog" processor cycles. This generally would mean that the Timer/Counter B3 interrupt should be disabled, eliminating the availability of the time functions. It can also affect adversely the *tone* function and the Servo library which expect the divisor to be /64.

A second problem with Timer/Counter B3 is that its ISR is part of the Arduino Library. Any attempt to replace it to fix the time functions with a different clock divisor would require rewriting and replacing wiring.c in the library. For that reason the best replacement would be to simply disable the B3 interrupt and using B2 for replacement time functions, if needed. B3 could be used for other functions not requiring an interrupt or output pin, perhaps using the event system.

The Servo library uses B2 which also expects TCA clock divider of /64. It would need modification to use another divisor. Consider using a PCA9685 for multiple servos rather than the software solution that uses B2.

However see the next section Chapter Sixteen - A Better Timer Setup (page 67) for Arduino library modifications that address some of these issues..

So let's look at the functionality of Timer/Counter B.

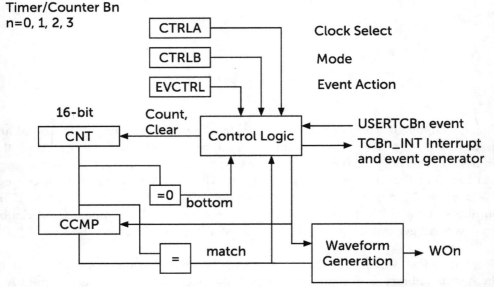

Timer/Counter Bn
n=0, 1, 2, 3

Each Timer/Counter B is independent and has two 16-bit registers, CNT and CCMP, as well as 6 useful control and status registers.

Control A Register TCBn.CTRLA

Bit	7	6	5	4	3	2	1	0
Function		RUNSTDBY		SYNCUPD		CLKSEL		ENABLE

RUNSTDBY allows the Timer/Counter to run in standby sleep mode. Only applies if CLKSEL is selecting a system clock. SYNCUPD restarts the Timer/Counter when TCA0 restarts or overflows, allowing synchronization with TCA. CLKSEL=2 uses the TCA0 clock divider as the clock source. CLKSEL=0 uses the system clock and CLKSEL=1 uses the system clock divided by 2. The Arduino library configures all TCBs to use the TCA0 clock divider except for the *tone* function on TCB1. The ENABLE bit turns on the Timer/Counter..

Control B Register TCBn.CTRLB

Bit	7	6	5	4	3	2	1	0
Function		ASYNC	CCMPINIT	CCMPEN		CNTMODE		

ASYNC enables asynchronous output in Single-Shot mode. CCMPINIT specifies the initial value of the output pin. CCMPEN enables the compare capture output, otherwise it is zero. On the Arduino board, the output of TCB0 is pin 6 and that of TCB1 is pin 3 with that of TCB2 and TCB3 inaccessible. The pin output is overridden so it is not necessary to set the pin to output. CNTMODE selects the Timer/Counter operating mode, all of which will be described later.

Value	Constant Name	Description
0	TCB_CNTMODE_INT_gc	Periodic Interrupt
1	TCB_CNTMODE_TIMEOUT_gc	Timeout Check
2	TCB_CNTMODE_CAPT_gc	Input Capture on Event
3	TCB_CNTMODE_FRQ_gc	I C Frequency Measurement
4	TCB_CNTMODE_PW_gc	I C Pulse-Width Measurement
5	TCB_CNTMODE_FRQPW_gc	I C Freq & Pulse-Width Measurement
6	TCB_CNTMODE_SINGLE_gc	Single-Shot
7	TCB_CNTMODE_PW8_gc	8-bit PWM

The output mode should not be changed with the Timer/Counter enabled. The Interrupt Flags register should also be cleared after configuring.

Event Control Register TCBn.EVCTRL

Bit	7	6	5	4	3	2	1	0
Function		FILTER		EDGE				CAPTEI

This register pertains to the Event System input, USERTCBn. FILTER enables noise cancelation — the input must be stable for four system clock cycles to indicate a change in input level. EDGE inverts the input. CAPTEI enables operation on input capture.

Interrupt Control and Flag Registers TCBn.INTCTRL and TCBn.INTFLAGS

Bit	7	6	5	4	3	2	1	0
Function								CAPT

The control register bit enables the capture interrupt, TCBn_INT. The flag register bit is cleared either by writing a "1" to it or by reading the CCMP register when in an Input Capture mode.

The interrupt flag is set (and an interrupt requested if the control bit is set) in a condition dependent on the operating mode. For the Periodic Interrupt, Timeout Check, and Single-Shot modes it is when CNT reaches CCMP. For 8-bit PWM mode it is when CNT reaches CCMPL. For the Input Capture on Event mode it is when the event occurs. For the Input Capture Frequency or Pulse-Width Measurement modes it is when the capture register (CCMP) is loaded. For the Input Capture Frequency and Pulse-Width Measurement mode it is on the second edge when the counter is stopped.

The condition that causes the interrupt flag to be set is also the trigger for the Event System generator EVSYS_GENERATOR_TCB*n*_CMP0_gc.

Status Register TCBn.STATUS

Bit	7	6	5	4	3	2	1	0
Function								RUN

The RUN bit is set if the counter is running. This bit is read-only.

Count Register TCBn.CNT
The CNT register is a 16 bit register with the counter value. The two halves can be read separately as CNTH and CNTL

Capture/Compare Register TCBn.CCMP
The CCMP register is a 16 bit register that holds the captured value of CNT in the Input Capture modes and the top CNT value in Periodic Interrupt, Time-Out, and Single-Shot modes. In the 8-bit PWM mode the upper and lower bytes, CCMPH and CCMPL are treated as separate 8-bit registers, with CCMPL holding the top value (setting the period) and CCMPH holding the comparison value (setting the duty cycle).

Example Programs
It would be remiss if there weren't an example program for each of the eight modes. To be aligned with the Arduino Library, the examples assume the TCA clock divider is always at /64 and the system clock speed is 16MHz. Timer/Counter B0 is used in all examples. When events are needed, they are generated using the *tone* or *analogWrite* functions. Only the setup/configuration code is shown here. Examine the programs for the full code.

Periodic Interrupt Mode
This is example program *TCB_INT*. The output pin is not used in this mode. An interrupt is triggered every CCMP+1 Timer/Counter clock periods. In this example the interrupt toggles pin 2 while the Event System routes the event to pin 5. The period is 10μs. The setup code is:

```
ddr.digital_2 = 1; // See interrupt on digital pin 2
EVSYS.CHANNEL0 = EVSYS_GENERATOR_TCB0_CMP0_gc; // Route output
EVSYS.USEREVOUTB = EVSYS_CHANNEL_CHANNEL0_gc; // to digital 5
ddr.digital_5 = 1;
TCB0.CTRLA = 0; // Turn off channel for configuring
TCB0.CTRLB = 0x0; // Periodic Interrupt Mode
TCB0.CCMP = 159; // 160 clocks per period, 10us
TCB0.INTCTRL = 1; // Enable interrupts
TCB0.CTRLA = 1; // Enable and use system clock
```

8-bit PWM Mode

This is example program *TCB_PWM*. The Arduino Library configures TCB0 and TCB1 for PWM using this mode. However in this example the full system clock speed is used, giving a 16μs period instead of a 1.024ms period. Output is used. Interrupts or the event system could be used as well but aren't in this example. TCB does not have the double buffering, so changing the duty cycle to a smaller value can cause a one cycle "hiccup" if the counter is already higher than the new duty cycle value. TCB2 is not suitable for this mode because the output pin is not brought out on the Arduino board. The setup code is:

```
TCB0.CTRLA = 0; // Turn off channel for configuring
TCB0.CTRLB = 0x17; // output enabled, PWM mode
TCB0.CCMPL = 0xff; // Maximum value will give 16us period
TCB0.CCMPH = 128; // 50% duty cycle
TCB0.CTRLA = 1; // Enable and use system clock
```

Single-Shot Mode

This is example program TCB_SINGLE. The *tone* function is used to generate a square wave on pin 3. The Event System is used to route that square wave directly to the event input of TCB0. TCB0 is configured to produce a 1μs pulse on the event. TCB2 is not suitable for this mode because the output pin is not brought out on the Arduino board. For reasons I don't understand, setting EDGE=1 causes the pulse to be generated on both edges of the square wave. It should cause the pulse to be generated on only the negative edge of the square wave. Is this an error in the part or in the documentation? In any case, here is the setup code:

```
tone(3, 1000); // 1kHz tone on pin 3
EVSYS.CHANNEL4 = EVSYS_GENERATOR_PORT1_PIN5_gc; // Route pin 3, PF5
EVSYS.USERTCB0 = EVSYS_CHANNEL_CHANNEL4_gc; // to TCB0
TCB0.CTRLA = 0; // Turn off channel for configuring
TCB0.CTRLB = 0x16; // Enable output, single shot mode
TCB0.EVCTRL = 0x41; // Enable input capture, rising edge of signal
TCB0.CNT = 15; // Prevents false first pulse
TCB0.CCMP = 15; // 16 clock (1us) pulse
TCB0.CTRLA = 1; // Enable and use system clock
```

Input Capture On Event Mode

This is example program *TCB_CAPT*. The *tone* function is used to generate a square wave on pin 3. The Event System is used to route that square wave directly to the event input of TCB0. The counter counts at full system clock speed. Every event the counter value is captured in CCMP and an interrupt occurs. The interrupt service routine calculates the difference of the CCMP value with that of the previous interrupt to measure the period of the square wave. The period in microseconds is printed to the terminal.

The setup code is:

```
tone(3, 1000); // 1kHz tone on pin 3
EVSYS.CHANNEL4 = EVSYS_GENERATOR_PORT1_PIN5_gc; // Route pin 3, PF5
EVSYS.USERTCB0 = EVSYS_CHANNEL_CHANNEL4_gc; // to TCB0
TCB0.CTRLA = 0; // Turn off channel for configuring
TCB0.CTRLB = 0x2; // capture on event mode
TCB0.EVCTRL = 0x41; // Enable input capture, rising edge of signal
TCB0.INTCTRL = 1; // Enable interrupt
TCB0.CTRLA = 1; // Enable and use system clock
```

Input Capture Pulse-Width Measurement Mode

This is example program *TCB_PW*. The *analogWrite* function is used to generate a pulse train alternating 256µs high and 768µs low. The Event System is used to route that waveform directly to the event input of TCB0. The counter counts at full system clock speed. The rising edge of the pulse starts the counter from zero. The falling edge saves the counter in CCMP and triggers an interrupt. The interrupt service routine copies the value in CCMP into a variable representing the pulse width which is then printed to the terminal. If the EDGE bit is set then the period of the negative pulse is measured. The setup code is:

```
analogWrite(3, 64); // 256us high, 768us low
EVSYS.CHANNEL4 = EVSYS_GENERATOR_PORT1_PIN5_gc; // Route pin 3, PF5
EVSYS.USERTCB0 = EVSYS_CHANNEL_CHANNEL4_gc; // to TCB0
TCB0.CTRLA = 0; // Turn off channel for configuring
TCB0.CTRLB = 0x4; // pulse width mode
TCB0.EVCTRL = 0x41; // Enable input capture, positive pulse
//  TCB0.EVCTRL = 0x51; // Enable input capture, negative pulse
TCB0.INTCTRL = 1; // Enable interrupt
TCB0.CTRLA = 1; // Enable and use system clock
```

Input Capture Time-Out Check Mode

This is example program *TCB_TIMEOUT*. This is similar to Pulse-Width Measurement mode however no measurement is actually made. The CCMP register is set to a value representing the maximum acceptable pulse width. If that value is exceeded an interrupt is triggered. The CCMP value is set for 500µs. If the positive pulse is being measured (256µs) then the interrupt is not triggered. If the negative pulse is being measured (768µs) then the interrupt is triggered. The interrupt routine must clear the interrupt flag.

The setup code is:
```
analogWrite(3, 64); // 256us high, 768us low
EVSYS.CHANNEL4 = EVSYS_GENERATOR_PORT1_PIN5_gc; // Route pin 3, PF5
EVSYS.USERTCB0 = EVSYS_CHANNEL_CHANNEL4_gc; // to TCB0
TCB0.CTRLA = 0; // Turn off channel for configuring
TCB0.CTRLB = 0x1; // time-out check mode
TCB0.CCMP = 500*16; // Time out at 500us
TCB0.EVCTRL = 0x41; // Enable input capture, positive pulse
// TCB0.EVCTRL = 0x51; // Enable input capture, negative pulse
TCB0.INTCTRL = 1; // Enable interrupt
TCB0.CTRLA = 1; // Enable and use system clock
```

Input Capture Frequency Measurement Mode

This is example program *TCB_FRQ*. However, only the rising edge (falling edge if EDGE=1) is used so the period is measured instead of pulse width. Note that the name of the mode is a misnomer. It's measuring the period and not the frequency. In the example program the *tone* function is used to create a 1kHz square wave, which the program measures the period to be $1000\mu s$. Functionally this gives the same result as the Input Capture on Event Mode example, however it takes less code to implement. The setup code is:
```
tone(3, 1000); // 1 kHz square wave on pin 3
EVSYS.CHANNEL4 = EVSYS_GENERATOR_PORT1_PIN5_gc; // Route pin 3, PF5
EVSYS.USERTCB0 = EVSYS_CHANNEL_CHANNEL4_gc; // to TCB0
TCB0.CTRLA = 0; // Turn off channel for configuring
TCB0.CTRLB = 0x3; // Frequency mode
TCB0.EVCTRL = 0x41; // Enable input capture, positive edge
// TCB0.EVCTRL = 0x51; // Enable input capture, negative edge
TCB0.INTCTRL = 1; // Enable interrupt
TCB0.CTRLA = 1; // Enable and use system clock
```

Input Capture Frequency and Pulse Width Measurement Mode

This is example program *TCB_FRQPW*. This combines the measurement of the pulse width (positive if EDGE=0, negative if EDGE=1) and frequency (actually period). The interrupt routine reads the period first from the CNT register then the pulse width from the CCMP register. Reading the CCMP register allows a new measurement to be made and clears the interrupt flag. The setup code is:
```
analogWrite(3, 64); // 256us high, 768us low, 1024us period
EVSYS.CHANNEL4 = EVSYS_GENERATOR_PORT1_PIN5_gc; // Route pin 3, PF5
EVSYS.USERTCB0 = EVSYS_CHANNEL_CHANNEL4_gc; // to TCB0
TCB0.CTRLA = 0; // Turn off channel for configuring
TCB0.CTRLB = 0x5; // frequency and pulse width mode
TCB0.EVCTRL = 0x41; // Enable input capture, positive pulse
// TCB0.EVCTRL = 0x51; // Enable input capture, negative pulse
TCB0.INTCTRL = 1; // Enable interrupt
TCB0.CTRLA = 1; // Enable and use system clock
```

CHAPTER SIXTEEN

A Better Timer Setup

This chapter is dedicated to improving the performance of Timer/Counter related functions by optimizing them for the ATmega4809. As has been stated before, design decisions were made to keep it as functionally compatible/identical with the ATmega328P in the Arduino Nano. Lets look at some specifications.

Arduino Nano PWM (analogWrite) Functions

Pin	PWM Frequency	Duty Cycle Settings	Dual Slope?
3	490 Hz (2.040ms)	(N/255)%	Yes
5	977 Hz (1.024ms)	N=0, 0%; N>0, ((N+1)/256)%	No
6	977	N=0, 0%; N>0, ((N+1)/256)%	No
9	490	(N/255)%	Yes
10	490	(N/255)%	Yes
11	490	(N/255)%	Yes

None of the PWM channels are double buffered, so can glitch if setting is changed
Note the nonlinearity of the *analogWrite* parameter for pins 5 and 6.

Arduino Nano Every PWM (analogWrite) Functions

Pin	PWM Frequency	Duty Cycle Settings	Double Buffered?
3	977 Hz (1.024ms)	0<=N<=256, (N/256)%	No
5	977 Hz (1.024ms)	0<=N<=256, (N/256)%	Yes
6	977 Hz (1.024ms)	0<=N<=256, (N/256)%	No
9	977 Hz (1.024ms)	0<=N<=256, (N/256)%	Yes
10	977 Hz (1.024ms)	0<=N<=256, (N/256)%	Yes

None of the PWM channels are Dual Slope.
Nano Every *analogWrite* function actually has parameter range 0 - 256, not 0 - 255, so is now linear.

Arduino Nano tone function goes down to 31Hz. The Servo library allows periods of up to 32.767ms using a clock divisor of 8. Resolution of servo pulses is 0.5μs

Arduino Nano Every tone function goes down to 2Hz (129Hz without using the prescaler).The Servo library allows periods of up to 262ms using a clock divisor of 64. Resolution of servo pulses is 4μs

In either case the micros function has a resolution of 4μs.

When using the 20MHz clock, all the frequencies are 25% higher. The micros function resolves to 3.2μs but returns values to the nearest microsecond so it will appear erratic.

If we change the prescaler to 8, we can make all frequencies 8 times higher. It appears to have no negative impact in comparison to the Arduino Nano. A prescaler of 4 would make the tone function worse at 20Mhz clock, and would make the period of the Servo library too short. However that would give better operation of micros with a 20MHz clock. While we are at it, we can optionally change pins 5, 9, and 10 to dual slope.

We will also run TCB3 on system clock/2 instead of using the TCA prescaler. That will make it possible to change the value of the TCA prescaler without impacting the time tracking functions.

Let's also get the ADC running at full speed. In the ATmega328P it runs at 125kHz. The same is true for the ATmega4809 even though it is capable of running at 1.5MHz. We can run it at 1MHz with the best choice prescaler, eight times faster. However the 0.55 volt reference cannot be used at this speed. Remember to lower the ADC clock speed when using the 0.55 volt reference.

The Modifications

The first thing I did was to add a defined symbol BETTER_OPERATION so I can conditionally compile the modifications. That way I can always revert to the standard library functions. Since the ATmega328P emulation is basically worthless, I rewrote the menu code in board.txt for both the nano4809 and fast4809. Example:

```
nona4809.menu.mode.on=Better Operation
nona4809.menu.mode.on.build.328emulation=-DBETTER_OPERATION
#nona4809.menu.mode.on=ATMEGA328
#nona4809.menu.mode.on.build.328emulation=-DAVR_NANO_4809_328MODE
nona4809.menu.mode.off=None (ATMEGA4809)
nona4809.menu.mode.off.build.328emulation=
```

I then determined that I needed to modify timers.h, wiring.c, Tone.cpp, variant.c and Servo.cpp, making sure to modify the versions of these files used by the megaavr cores, and not those used by the Arduino Nano.

The example program distribution has the modified files that you can use freely. Note that these are modifications of Arduino megaAVR Boards version 1.8.6 and the Servo library version 1.1.6. If you are using another version, check the files closely before replacing, possibly just putting the modifications in your existing library files. You should save the original files in a safe location in case you want to revert the changes. The new code is shown below, but the deleted code can only be seen in the replacement source files.

nona4809/timers.h

This file defines some time tracking (*millis*, *micros*, ...) constants. To simplify operation, we will have the TCB3 period be exactly 1ms. This means with a 16MHz clock and the /8 prescaler we need 2000 counts per interrupt. With a 20MHz clock we need 2500 counts per interrupt.

```
#if F_CPU == 20000000L // 20 MHz
#define TIME_TRACKING_TIMER_PERIOD    9999  // To get exactly 1ms with
the /2 prescaler
#else // 16 MHz
#define TIME_TRACKING_TIMER_PERIOD    7999  // To get exactly 1ms with
the /2 prescaler
#endif
#define TIME_TRACKING_TICKS_PER_OVF   (TIME_TRACKING_TIMER_PERIOD +
1)  // Timer ticks per overflow of TCB3
#define TIME_TRACKING_TIMER_DIVIDER   2   // Clock divider for TCB3
#define TIME_TRACKING_CYCLES_PER_OVF  (TIME_TRACKING_TICKS_PER_OVF *
TIME_TRACKING_TIMER_DIVIDER)
```

nona4809/variant.c

The file has the function *setup_timers* and the timers do need to be set up differently.

We need to change the prescaler.
```
// Use DIV8 prescaler (giving 2MHz clock), enable TCA timer
TCA0.SINGLE.CTRLA = (TCA_SINGLE_CLKSEL_DIV8_gc) |
                    (TCA_SINGLE_ENABLE_bm);
```

For the Type A PWM functions, we want to use dual slope PWM. Don't make this change if you want to still use single slope PWM.
```
// Setup timers for dual slope PWM,
// but do not enable, will do in analogWrite()
TCA0.SINGLE.CTRLB = TCA_SINGLE_WGMODE_DSBOTTOM_gc;

// Period setting, 16 bit register but val resolution is 8 bit
TCA0.SINGLE.PER = PWM_TIMER_PERIOD + 1;
```

arduino/wiring.c

For this change, and the ones that follow, make sure the file is the one in the megaavr tree. The first change here is to replace the ADC prescaler setup code to get 1 to 1.25 MHz operation.

```
#if F_CPU >= 20000000 // 20 MHz / 16 = 1.25MHz
        ADC0.CTRLC |= ADC_PRESC_DIV16_gc;
#elif F_CPU >= 16000000 // 16 MHz / 16 = 1MHz
        ADC0.CTRLC |= ADC_PRESC_DIV16_gc;
#elif F_CPU >= 8000000 // 8 MHz / 8 = 1 MHz
        ADC0.CTRLC |= ADC_PRESC_DIV8_gc;
#elif F_CPU >= 4000000 // 4 MHz / 4 = 1 MHz
        ADC0.CTRLC |= ADC_PRESC_DIV4_gc;
#else // 2MHz or slower  2 MHz / 2 = 1MHz kHz
        ADC0.CTRLC |= ADC_PRESC_DIV2_gc;
#endif
```

The changes to the TCB3_INT interrupt service routine and the micros function were so extensive I simply rewrote them. The original code could not handle timer ticks faster than 1MHz and has now unnecessary code to handle interrupt periods other than 1ms. The change meant that the following variables could be eliminated: *microseconds_per_timer_overflow, microseconds_per_timer_tick, millis_inc, fract_inc, FRACT_MAX, timer_fract,* and *timer_overflow_count.* The ISR becomes:

```
ISR(TCB3_INT_vect)
{
// We know that there will be no fraction because interrupt is exactly
at 1ms intervals
// So we can simplify this code a great deal
        timer_millis++;

        /* Clear flag */
        _timer->INTFLAGS = TCB_CAPT_bm;
}
```

The *micros* function becomes:

```
unsigned long micros() {
        unsigned long overflows, microseconds;
        uint16_t ticks;
        /* Save current state and disable interrupts */
        uint8_t status = SREG;
        cli();

        /* Get current number of overflows and timer count */
        overflows = timer_millis;
        ticks = _timer->CNT;

        /* If the timer overflow flag is raised, we just missed it,
        increment to account for it, & read new ticks */
        if(_timer->INTFLAGS & TCB_CAPT_bm){
                overflows++;
```

```
        ticks = _timer->CNT;
    }
    /* Restore state */
    SREG = status;

    /* Return microseconds of up time  (resets every ~70mins) */
    #if F_CPU == 20000000L // A clock tick is 100ns
    microseconds = overflows*1000 + (((uint32_t)ticks*6554) >> 16);
//  microseconds = overflows*1000 + ticks/10;
    #else // a clock tick 125ns
    microseconds = overflows*1000 + (ticks >> 3);
    #endif
    return microseconds;
}
```

The expression *ticks/10* requires a slow division. The micros function doubles in speed with the approximation to /10 of *6554 >> 16, which eliminates the need for a divide. The slight error is undetectable with the value of ticks in the range 0 to 9999.

The *init* function, besides the change to the ADC clock configuration, has lines to set the variables *microseconds_per_timer_overflow, microseconds_per_timer_tick, millis_inc*, and *fract_inc* which are no longer needed. But there is a comment stating that we are in the default Periodic Interrupt Mode, which is not the case. It was in 8 bit PWM like the other TCB channels. So we need to set the correct mode:

```
    _timer->CTRLB = (TCB_CNTMODE_INT_gc);
                    // Not really the default, so set it!
```

We also need to change TCB3 to use the system clock /2 rather than TCA prescaler:

```
    /* Clock selection -> system clock /2, 8MHz or 10Mhz */
    _timer->CTRLA = TCB_CLKSEL_CLKDIV2_gc;
```

arduino/Tone.cpp

The tone function needs to be changed where it sets the compare value. The new code is:

```
    // If compare larger than 16bits, need to prescale (will be DIV8)
    uint8_t prescaler_needed = 0;
    if (compare_val > 0xFFFF){
        // recalculate with new prescaler
        compare_val = F_CPU_CORRECTED / frequency / 2 / 8 - 1;
        prescaler_needed = 1;
    }
```

megaavr/Servo.cpp

The servo library doesn't work for the 20MHz clock even without BETTER_OPERATION, and the calculation of the period was done wrong when they translated the library for the ATmega4809. At some time in the future, they may rewrite the *ServoHandler* function to correct the error, but I've already done so here. New definitions (actually the old ATmega328P definitions) needed for *usToTicks* and *ticksToUs* and a casting was added to prevent overflow with the 20MHz clock:

```
#ifdef BETTER_OPERATION
#define usToTicks(_us)      (( clockCyclesPerMicrosecond()* (unsigned
long) _us) / 8)      // converts microseconds to tick (assumes prescale
of 8)
#define ticksToUs(_ticks) (( (unsigned)_ticks * 8)/
clockCyclesPerMicrosecond() ) // converts from ticks back to
microseconds
#else
// Cast to long was needed to prevent overflow with 20MHz clock
#define usToTicks(_us)      ((clockCyclesPerMicrosecond() / 4 *
(unsigned long)_us) / 16)                    // converts microseconds to
tick
#define ticksToUs(_ticks) (((unsigned) _ticks * 16) /
(clockCyclesPerMicrosecond() / 4))    // converts from ticks back to
microseconds
#endif
```

The error with *ServoHandler* was a result of the different counter operation. The fix has variable *tcCounterValue* to hold the count after the start of the period, much like the hardware counter did in the ATmega328P. This allows the correct computation of the remaining period after the final pulse in the period. It used to just make the remaining period about 16ms. The entire library should be cleaned up to not use a step size of 4μs, but I'll leave that to someone else. See the example program distribution for the revised function and file.

The resulting specifications are:

Modified Arduino Nano Every PWM (analogWrite) Functions

Pin	PWM Frequency	Duty Cycle Settings	Dual Slope, Double Buffered
3	7.81 kHz (128μs)	0<=N<=256, (N/256)%	No
5	3.91 kHz (256μs)	0<=N<=256, (N/256)%	Yes
6	7.81 kHz (128μs)	0<=N<=256, (N/256)%	No
9	3.91 kHz (256μs)	0<=N<=256, (N/256)%	Yes
10	3.91 kHz (256μs)	0<=N<=256, (N/256)%	Yes

The tone function goes down to 16Hz. The micros function resolves to $1\mu s$. The ADC is 8 times faster. The Servo library is back to periods of up to 32.767ms with resolution of servo pulses being $0.5\mu s$.

Again, with the 20MHz clock, all frequencies and periods are 25% faster. However the micros function itself takes longer to execute because it needs to do a division.

As a bonus, using BETTER_OPERATION saves both program memory and RAM.

CHAPTER SEVENTEEN
Watchdog Timer

The Watchdog Timer (WDT) in the ATmega4809 has a new windowing capability where the reset must occur within a window of time. It also no longer has the interrupt instead of reset mode, but there are other timers that can be used instead for long period interrupts we will look at in the next chapter.

To use the WDT, include *avr/wdt.h* to get the definition of *wdt_reset()*, which executes the instruction that resets the WDT. The WDT has two registers:

Control A Register WDT.CTRLA

Bit	7	6	5	4	3	2	1	0
Function	WINDOW				PERIOD			

Writing a non-zero value to PERIOD enables the WDT and sets the period before the WDT system reset occurs. *wdt_reset* must be called before this time to prevent the system reset. The following time selections are available. Note that the WDT uses a special low-power, slow speed clock that isn't accurate.

Value	Constant	Description
0	WDT_PERIOD_OFF_gc	Off
1	WDT_PERIOD_8CLK_gc	8ms
2	WDT_PERIOD_16CLK_gc	16ms
3	WDT_PERIOD_32CLK_gc	32ms
4	WDT_PERIOD_64CLK_gc	64ms
5	WDT_PERIOD_128CLK_gc	128ms
6	WDT_PERIOD_256CLK_gc	256ms
7	WDT_PERIOD_512CLK_gc	512ms
8	WDT_PERIOD_1KCLK_gc	1.024s
9	WDT_PERIOD_2KCLK_gc	2.048s
10	WDT_PERIOD_4KCLK_gc	4.096s
11	WDT_PERIOD_8KCLK_gc	8.192s

Writing a non-zero value to WINDOW puts the WDT in window mode. If the WDT is reset within the WINDOW time of the previous reset then a WDT system reset will occur. After the WINDOW period, then the WDT may be reset for the PERIOD period. After WINDOW plus PERIOD times have passed without reset, the WDT system reset will occur. The first windowing period occurs after the first call to *wdt_reset*. The same time choices are available:

Value	Constant	Description
0	WDT_WINDOW_OFF_gc	Off
1	WDT_WINDOW_8CLK_gc	8ms
2	WDT_WINDOW_16CLK_gc	16ms
3	WDT_WINDOW_32CLK_gc	32ms
4	WDT_WINDOW_64CLK_gc	64ms
5	WDT_WINDOW_128CLK_gc	128ms
6	WDT_WINDOW_256CLK_gc	256ms
7	WDT_WINDOW_512CLK_gc	512ms
8	WDT_WINDOW_1KCLK_gc	1.024s
9	WDT_WINDOW_2KCLK_gc	2.048s
10	WDT_WINDOW_4KCLK_gc	4.096s
11	WDT_WINDOW_8KCLK_gc	8.192s

Because of a protection mechanism, this register cannot be changed if the LOCK bit in WDT.STATUS is set. Also the register cannot be changed without writing a special key value to the CPU_CCP (Configuration Change Protection) register within 4 CPU instructions before writing to the CTRLA register. Writing to the CCP register automatically disables interrupts for the 4 CPU instructions, so interrupts do not have to be explicitly disabled when setting the WDT registers.

Status Register WDT.STATUS

Bit	7	6	5	4	3	2	1	0
Function	LOCK							SYNCBUSY

The LOCK bit prevents writing to either the CTRLA or STATUS registers. Like the CTRLA register, this register cannot be changed without writing a special key value to the CPU_CCP register within 4 CPU instructions before writing to the STATUS register. The SYNCBUSY bit is read-only and indicates that the data just written to the CTRLA register is being transferred to the WDT clock domain. The WDT doesn't start until this bit has returned to 0. A *wdt_reset* will be ignored while this bit is 1.

The example program *WDT* demonstrates operation of the Watchdog Timer. It is equivalent to the *watchdog_reset* example program for the ATmega328P in the *Far Inside The Arduino* book, but for adding a window. If RESETTOOSOON is not defined, the program will run for 2.25 seconds after the second *wdt_reset* and then the system reset occurs and the process repeats. If RESETTOOSOON is defined, then the second *wdt_reset* occurs 200ms after the first, which causes a system reset "too soon", and the process repeats.

Setup code for the WDT is:
```
CPU_CCP = CCP_IOREG_gc; // allow changes
WDT.CTRLA = WDT_WINDOW_256CLK_gc | WDT_PERIOD_2KCLK_gc;
          // 256ms window 2 second period
CPU_CCP = CCP_IOREG_gc; // allow changes
WDT.STATUS = WDT_LOCK_bm; // lock it
while (WDT.STATUS & WDT_SYNCBUSY_bm != 0)
{} ; // wait for synchronizing complete
wdt_reset(); // first reset enables windowing
```

CHAPTER EIGHTEEN

Other Timers

The older AVR microcontrollers provided a Watchdog timer that could be configured as a slow periodic interrupt rather than the traditional watchdog function. In the ATmega4809, the watchdog timer is just a watchdog timer. However the microcontroller has two new timer/counters, the Real-Time Counter (RTC) and the Periodic Interrupt Timer (PIT). These use the same clock source but are otherwise independent.

Internal or external clock sources can be selected. External sources are not really practical on the Arduino board. The internal clock source is a 32.684kHz oscillator, however there is also optional /32 prescaler that gives a 1.024kHz clock. The clock must be configured before enabling the RTC or PIT.

Clock Selection Register RTC.CLKSEL

Bit	7	6	5	4	3	2	1	0
Function							CLKSEL	

The value 0 selects the 32.768kHz internal oscillator. The value 1 selects the prescaler and the internal oscillator giving a frequency of 1.024kHz. Selections 2 and 3 are for external oscillators and won't be discussed here.

Real-Time Counter

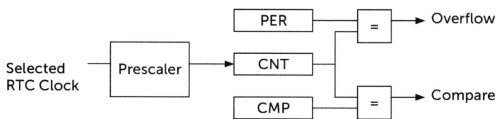

The Real-Time counter has a clock prescaler and three 16-bit registers. CNT is the counter which increments with every clock tick. PER is the period. When CNT reaches PER the overflow interrupt is triggered and the counter resets to zero. The actual period is PER+1 ticks. CMP is a compare register. When CNT equals CMP the Compare interrupt is triggered.

Control A Register RTC.CTRLA

Bit	7	6	5	4	3	2	1	0
Function	RUNSTDBY	PRESCALER				CORREN		RTCEN

RUNSTDBY enables running in standby sleep mode. CORREN enables frequency correction. This is useful to calibrate external crystal clock sources for extra accuracy. RTCEN enables the Real-Time Counter. The PRESCALER has 16 settings, where the clock division is $1/(2^{PRESCALER})$. So a value 0 zero turns the prescaler off. The maximum value of 15 will divide by 32,768, giving a 1Hz clock rate when the internal 32.768kHz clock is selected. The prescaler should not be changed if the CTRLABUSY flag is set in the status register.

Status Register RTC.STATUS

Bit	7	6	5	4	3	2	1	0
Function					CMPBUSY	PERBUSY	CNTBUSY	CTRLABUSY

Because the RTC clock is asynchronous to the system clock, and is much slower, writing to the registers occur after a varying amount of delay. The flag bits indicate that the particular register is busy writing the previous value. Do not write to these registers if their busy flag is set but wait for the bit to clear first. It is best to set these registers up before enabling the RTC, then there will be no issues.

Interrupt Control and Flag Registers RTC.INTCTRL and RTC.INTFLAGS

Bit	7	6	5	4	3	2	1	0
Function							CMP	OVF

The CMP control bit enables the interrupt for compare match while the OVF bit enables the interrupt for counter overflow and reset. There is a single interrupt vector RTC_CNT for both. The flag register is read to determine the source of the interrupt. To clear a flag bit, write a "1" to it.

Setting of the flags also create events. OVF causes the event
EVSYS_GENERATOR_RTC_OVF
and CMP causes the event
EVSYS_GENERATOR_RTC_CMP.

Count, Period, and Compare Registers RTC.CNT, RTC.PER, RTC.CMP

These 16 bit registers should only be written if their corresponding STATUS register bit is 0. It is best to load these before enabling the RTC.

Periodic Interrupt Timer

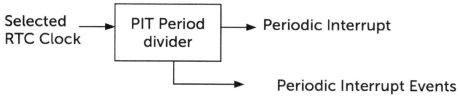

The Periodic Interrupt Timer divides the selected RTC Clock and generates an interrupt. The divider can be set to /4 to /32768. Additionally events can be generated at rates between /64 and /8192.

Periodic Interrupt Timer Control A Register RTC.PITCTRLA

Bit	7	6	5	4	3	2	1	0
Function		PERIOD						PITEN

The PERIOD field values of 1 through 14 select the divider to be $1/(2^{(PERIOD+1)})$. A value of 0 turns the periodic interrupt off. PITEN enables the Periodic Interrupt Timer.

Periodic Event Timer events are generated as described in the section on the Chapter Nine - Event System (page 23). There are four events, EVSYS_GENERATOR_PIT0 through PIT3, each representing a different division factor depending on the channel. All powers of two from /64 through /8192 are available.

Periodic Interrupt Timer Status Register RTC.PITSTATUS

Bit	7	6	5	4	3	2	1	0
Function								CTRLBUSY

As with the Real-Time Counter, do not write to the PITCTRLA register if the CTRLBUSY bit in the PITSTATUS register is 1.

Periodic Interrupt Timer Interrupt Control and Flag Registers RTC.PITINTCTRL and RTC.PITINTFLAGS

Bit	7	6	5	4	3	2	1	0
Function								PI

The PI control bit enables the Periodic Interrupt Timer Interrupt, RTC_PIT. The flag bit is cleared by writing a "1" to it.

The example program, *RTC*, uses both the Real-Time Counter and the Programmable Interrupt Timer interrupts, but not the Event System. The Real-Time Counter is used to display "Tick" "Tock" in the terminal. Tock is displayed when the counter period of one second is reached while Tick is displayed when the counter value equals a half second. The LED flashes on or off twice a second and is driven by the Periodic Interrupt Timer. Setup of the module is:

```
RTC.CLKSEL = 0; // Internal 32.768kHz clock
RTC.PER = 32767; // Gives a period of 32768
RTC.CMP = 16384; // Compare half way through
RTC.INTCTRL = 3; // Enable both CMP and OVF interrupts
RTC.CTRLA = 1; // Enable RTC, prescaler is off
RTC.PITINTCTRL = 1; // Enable PI interrupt
RTC.PITCTRLA = RTC_PERIOD_CYC16384_gc + 1;
                // This will be half a second. Enable PIT
```

The interrupt routines are:

```
ISR(RTC_CNT_vect) {
  if ((RTC.INTFLAGS & 1) != 0) { // OVF
    RTC.INTFLAGS = 1; // clear interrupt
    Serial.println("...Tock");
  } else if ((RTC.INTFLAGS & 2) != 0) { // CMP
    RTC.INTFLAGS = 2; // clear interrupt
    Serial.print("Tick...");
  }
}

ISR(RTC_PIT_vect) {
  pin.digital_13 = 1; // Toggle LED
  RTC.PITINTFLAGS = 1; // clear interrupt
}
```

CHAPTER NINETEEN

SPI

The good news about the SPI interface in the ATmega4809 is that the transmit and receive data are now buffered. This vastly eliminates the possibility of data loss when operating as a slave, a problem with the ATmega328P discussed in *Far Inside The Arduino*. With buffering disabled, writing to the data register writes directly to the shift register. There is a single buffer register for the receiver which allows reading data shifted in after the next shifting begins, but not before it finishes. With buffering enabled, there is an added transmit buffer register allowing writing to the data register while the previous byte is being shifted. And enabled buffering adds a second receive buffer register, the receive buffers acting like a two stage FIFO.

Buffering Off

Buffering On

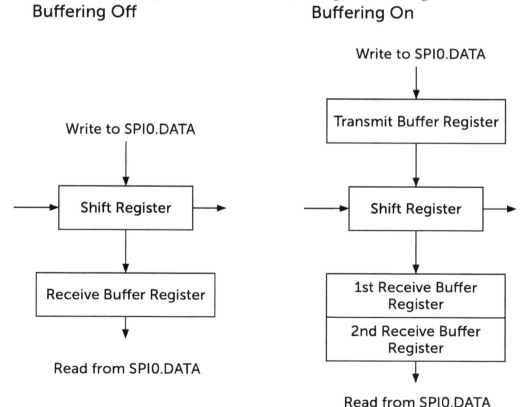

Except for the buffering, there is no functional difference of the SPI between the ATmega4809 and ATmega328P. The extra buffering is especially useful when operating as a slave. But we will look at use as a master with buffering disabled. Comparing the Arduino Nano Every board to the Arduino Nano or Uno boards, the new Every has the SS signal on pin 8 instead of 10. The other pins are the same: MOSI on pin 11, MISO on pin 12, and SCK on pin 13 (shared with the LED). This is good since pin 10 can be used for PWM while pin 8 has no special use other than as an additional analog input. The device registers are different between the two parts. Remember that the port multiplexer must be configured so that the SPI signals are connected to the correct pins on the Arduino Nano Every. This can be done with the statement:

```
PORTMUX.TWISPIROUTEA |= PORTMUX_SPI0_ALT2_gc;
```

Control A Register SPI0.CTRLA

Bit	7	6	5	4	3	2	1	0
Function		DORD	MASTER	CLK2X		PRESC1	PRESC0	ENABLE

The DORD bit selects the LSB of the data to be transmitted first, otherwise the MSB is transmitted first. The MASTER bit puts the SPI interface in MASTER mode. The ENABLE bit enables the SPI. The CLK2X and PRESC bits select the SPI prescaler division factor according to this table:

CLK2X	PRESC1	PRESC0	Division Factor
0	0	0	4
0	0	1	16
0	1	0	64
0	1	1	128
1	0	0	2
1	0	1	8
1	1	0	32
1	1	1	64

In master mode the direction of the MOSI and SCK pins must be set to be output pins. The SS functionality is controlled manually in software and doesn't really have to be on the assigned pin. However the multi-master functionality will interpret a low input on the SS pin 8 to be a request for bus control and the MASTER bit will be cleared. For that reason pin 8 should be used only as an output pin if it is not used for the SS function. However, see the new SSD bit in the CTRLB register for a workaround.

Control B Register SPI0.CTRLB

Bit	7	6	5	4	3	2	1	0
Function	BUFEN	BUFWR				SSD	MODE1	MODE0

BUFEN enables buffer mode, which will be discussed with the operation as a slave. BUFWR is part of buffer mode operation and, if 0, will cause the first byte transferred out to be dummy data. If 1, the first write to the data register goes immediately to the shift register. Most applications will want this to be 1. The SSD bit, if 1, disables the multi-master capability allowing pin 8 to be used as an input pin in master mode. The MODE1 bit is the same as CPOL in other microcontrollers and the MODE0 bit is the same as CPHA. MODE1=1 is for negative going clock pulses instead of positive going clock pulses. CPHA is phase selection. CPHA=0 samples on the leading edge of the clock pulse while CPHA=1 samples on the trailing edge. Data is shifted on the opposite edge.

Interrupt Control Register SPI0.INTCTRL

Bit	7	6	5	4	3	2	1	0
Function	RXCIE	TXCIE	DREIE	SSIE				IE

Their are four interrupt conditions in buffered mode and a single condition for non-buffered mode. In either case there is a single interrupt vector, SPI0_INT. When in buffered mode RXCIE enables an interrupt when RXCIF interrupt flag is set, TXCIE enables an interrupt when TXCIF is set, DREIE enables an interrupt when DREIF is set, and SSIE enables an interrupt when SSIF is set. When in non-buffered mode, IE enables an interrupt when IF is set.

Interrupt Flags Register SPI0.INTFLAGS non-buffered mode

Bit	7	6	5	4	3	2	1	0
Function	IF	WRCOL						

IF is the Receive Complete interrupt flag. It is set when a byte has been completely shifted in/out of the data register SPI0.DATA. The bit is cleared by writing a "1" to it. The documentation states that the bit is cleared automatically upon entering the interrupt service routine, but I've found that isn't the case. It can also be cleared by reading the register while the bit is set and then accessing the data register. The WRCOL bit is set if the data register is written while data is still being shifted. It can be cleared by reading the flag register while the bit is set and then accessing the data register. Properly coded programs should not be writing to the data register unless it is known that the shifting is complete, which is indicated by the IF bit being set.

Interrupt Flags Register SPI0.INTFLAGS buffered mode

Bit	7	6	5	4	3	2	1	0
Function	RXCIF	TXCIF	DREIF	SSIF				BUFOVF

There is a single transmit buffer register, allowing storing the next byte to shift out while the current byte is being shifted out. There are two receive buffer registers, which act as a FIFO. This allows reading the most recent two bytes shifted in while a shift of a third byte is still occurring. This gives more time to handle incoming data. The flags give a better indication of the state of the buffers than a single flag bit would.

RXCIF, receive complete interrupt flag, is set when there is unread data in the receive buffer and cleared when it is empty. Read the data register to empty the receive buffer if there is data in it. This is the way to clear the flag in an SPI interrupt service routine. The documentation states the flag can also be cleared by writing a "1" to it, but, frankly, this doesn't make sense.

TXCIF, transfer complete interrupt flag, is set when there is no data in the transmit buffer to shift out and any shifting is complete. The flag is cleared by writing a "1" to it.

DREIF, data register empty interrupt flag, is set when the transmit is empty and ready to receive data. It is cleared when there is data in the buffer that hasn't been moved to the shift register. The bit is cleared by writing to the data register. When using an interrupt service routine, if there is no more data to transmit the DREIE interrupt must be disabled.

SSIF, slave select trigger interrupt flag, is set when the SPI is in master mode, the SS pin is configured as an input pin, SSD=0. and the pin has been pulled low (multiple master mode). The flag is cleared by writing a "1" to it.

BUFOVF, buffer overflow flag, is set when the receive buffer is full and a third byte has been shifted in, and a fourth byte is started to be shifted in. The flag is cleared by reading the data register.

Data Register SPI0.DATA
The data register reads and writes from two separate locations, and the locations depend on if buffering is enabled or disabled. When read, it reads from the receive buffer, which "pops" the FIFO if in buffered mode. When writing, it writes to the shift register if not buffered or the transmit buffer if buffered In either case, if the SPI is in master mode, it initiates shifting.

Example Program for SPI Master

An SPI exercise without an external component is somewhat meaningless and won't really prove it works. So the SPI is connected to an external shift register:

Nano Every

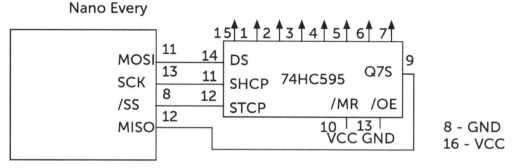

The example program, *SPI_MASTER*, uses the interrupt service routine to transfer all but the first byte of data. Even though the shift register only holds a single byte, three will be sent and three received. The three bytes sent are 0x55, 0xaa, and a value that increments with each three byte transfer. That third value will be stored in the shift register when SS goes high at the end of the transfer. The bytes received will be the one in the shift register, 0x55, and 0xaa in that order. The oscilloscope image shows, from top to bottom, SS, SCK, MOSI, and MISO.

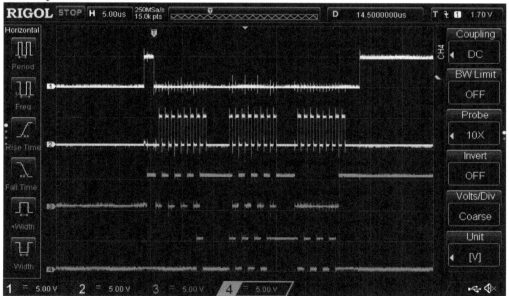

Setup code for the SPI:
```
PORTMUX.TWISPIROUTEA |= PORTMUX_SPI0_ALT2_gc;
ddr.digital_8 = 1; // SS pin
port.digital_8 = 1; // Normally high
ddr.digital_11 = 1; // MOSI pin
//ddr.digital_12 = 0; // MISO pin
ddr.digital_13 = 1; // SCK
SPI0.CTRLA = 0x23; // MASTER, /16, ENABLE
SPI0.CTRLB = 0; // Buffering off, CPOL=0, CPHA=0
SPI0.INTCTRL = 1; // Enable interrupt
```

There is an array holding the data to be sent, *dataOut,* and one for the data being received, *dataIn.* The variable *dataIndex* is the index into the arrays for the current transfer. The transfer is started with:
```
dataIndex = 0;
port.digital_8 = 0; // Enable SS
SPI0.DATA = dataOut[0]; // transmit first byte.
```

The ISR does the remaining transfers:
```
ISR(SPI0_INT_vect) { // receive and transmit bytes
  dataIn[dataIndex] = SPI0.DATA; // receive next byte
  dataIndex++;
  if (dataIndex < 3) { // more to send
    SPI0.DATA = dataOut[dataIndex];
  } else {
    port.digital_8 = 1; // Disable SS
  }
  SPI0.INTFLAGS = 0x80; // Reset interrupt flag
}
```

Example Programs for SPI Slave

The example programs for slave operation has a problem in that an SPI master is needed. The program can implement an SPI master in software. This is not ideal since we really want the master and slave operating asynchronously. So there is an additional program *SPI_DRIVER* that can be run on another Arduino board. It is a functionally equivalent master program using the SPI interface and the Arduino library so it should work on any other Arduino board you have. I have tested this on a Arduino Uno. The master SPI software can be disabled in the example programs by commenting out the define for *MASTER_TOO.*

Every example program resets the SPI by disabling and reenabling at the end of each completed transfer. While not always necessary, that keeps the master and slave in sync.

The master and slave SPI must be connected together, like functions to each other. When using the software master, connect pin 2 to 11 (MOSI), 3 to 12 (MISO), 4 to 8

(SS), and 5 to 13 (SCK). The SPI_DRIVER program uses the standard pins on the board for MISO, MOSI, and SCK, and pin 2 for SS. Connecting the Uno to the Nano Every, connect 11 to 11, 12 to 12, 13 to 13, and 2 on the Uno to 8 on the Nano Every. Be sure to connect the grounds of both boards together as well.

The master program shifts out four bytes, 0x55, 0xaa, 0x21, and 0x31 in that order, each byte LSB first. CPHA and CPOL both 0. It then prints out the four bytes it receives to the terminal. The returned values depend on what the slave does with the data.

The first slave program, *SPI_SLAVE_UNBUFFERED*, operates the slave SPI in unbuffered mode. The slave holds two bytes. Four bytes of data are shifted for each transfer. The first two bytes are shifted through the slave while the last two bytes end up in the slave at the end of the transfer. On the master receiving end, the first two bytes received are those from the slave while the last two are the ones sent from the master at the start of the transfer. The slave "processes" it's data by multiplying the two bytes together and sending out the product in the next transfer. The data printed by the master should be 0x06, 0x51, 0x55, 0xaa.

This is essentially the SPI slave example from *Far Inside The Arduino*, but for the ATmega4809 microcontroller. There are two variables, *inm1* and *inm2* to hold the last two bytes shifted in.

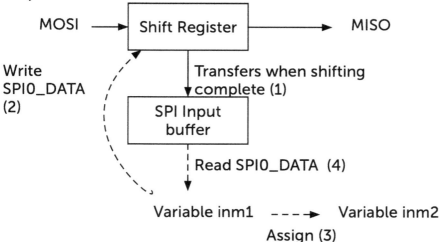

The data shifted in goes into the input buffer and causes an interrupt. The ISR writes *inm1* to the shift register, copies *inm1* to *inm2,*, and then reads the input buffer into *inm1*. The use of inm1 gives the two byte buffer/delay in passing through data. However there is a potential problem in that the SPI0.DATA register must be written before the next shift starts. This tends to make this program unreliable. In fact to have it work at all a delay is needed between bytes being shifted to allow the ISR to execute. In the SPI_DRIVER program there is a 1ms delay that must be uncommented for this program to work. Because the only indication that shifting has completed is the rising edge of SS, there is a second ISR for the GPIO pin interrupt that is triggered on the rising edge of SS. It is used to process the data and reset the SPI for the next transfer.

The configuration code in the setup function is:

```
PORTMUX.TWISPIROUTEA |= PORTMUX_SPI0_ALT2_gc; // Port Multiplexer
ddr.SLAVE_MISO = 1; // Config output pins
PORTE.PIN3CTRL = PORT_ISC_RISING_gc;
                    // Slave SS pin interrupts on rising edge
SPI0.CTRLA = 0x41; // Enable in slave mode, LSB first
SPI0.CTRLB = 0; // Buffering off, CPOL=0, CPHA=0
SPI0.INTCTRL = 1; // Enable interrupt
```

The SPI ISR performs the data manipulation shown in the figure above:

```
ISR(SPI0_INT_vect) { // A byte has come in
  SPI0.DATA = inm1;
  inm2 = inm1;
  inm1 = SPI0.DATA;
  SPI0.INTFLAGS = 0x80; // Reset interrupt flag
}
```

The interrupt for the rising edge of SS must first check for the final byte of data being available in case this ISR runs before the final SPI ISR. This ISR is:

```
ISR(PORTE_PORT_vect) { // Interrupt vector for SS rising
  if (intflg.SLAVE_SS != 0) { // SS rising
    while ((SPI0.INTFLAGS & 0x80) != 0) {
      // there is a pending SPI interrupt,
      // so do what it would have done
      //      SPI0.DATA = inm1; // No reason to do this
      inm2 = inm1;
      inm1 = SPI0.DATA;
    }
    // Reset the SPI
    SPI0.CTRLA &= ~1;
    // Values here are correct!
    // Our values are in inm2 (first received)
    // and inm1 (most recent received)
    // Let's return the product of the two bytes.
    uint16_t product = inm2 * inm1;
    inm1 = (uint8_t)(product & 0xff);
    inm2 = (uint8_t)(product >> 8);
    SPI0.CTRLA |= 1; // Turn SPI back on.
    // We put the most significant byte in SPI0.DATA
    // and the least is in inm1
    SPI0.DATA = inm2;
    intflg.SLAVE_SS = 1; // reset pin interrupt flag
  }
}
```

The first example program for buffered mode slave operation is *SPI_SLAVE_BUFFERED*. This program assumes it is the only slave device so doesn't pass through any data. It processes the four bytes shifted in by adding one to each byte. Then on the next transfer it shifts the four processed bytes out. This should be 0x56, 0xab, 0x22, and 0x32 in that order. Again, two ISRs are used. The SPI ISR is triggered when either RXCIF is set signaling data is available to read or DREIF is set signaling there is available room in the transmit buffer. The SPI0.DATA register is only accessed from this ISR. The pin interrupt ISR is used to process the data and reset the SPI.

The configuration code in the setup function is:

```
PORTMUX.TWISPIROUTEA |= PORTMUX_SPI0_ALT2_gc;
ddr.SLAVE_MISO = 1; // Config output pins
PORTE.PIN3CTRL = PORT_ISC_RISING_gc;
                   // Slave SS pin interrupts on rising edge
SPI0.CTRLA = 0x41; // Enable in slave mode, LSB first
SPI0.CTRLB = 0xc0; // Enable buffering
SPI0.INTCTRL = 0xA0;
    // Interrupt when receive buffer has content or send buffer empty
```

Data memory is defined:

```
volatile uint8_t receiveBuffer[4];
volatile uint8_t sendBuffer[4];
volatile uint8_t receiveIndex,sendIndex; //Index above next byte
```

The SPI ISR tosses out any extra incoming data. This should not happen and really indicates an error. When all four bytes have been sent, the interrupt on DREIF is disabled. The SPI ISR is:

```
volatile uint8_t dummy;

ISR(SPI0_INT_vect) { // We might be able to send or receive
  if ((SPI0.INTFLAGS & 0x20) != 0) { // transmit data register empty
    if (sendIndex < 4) { // more to send
      SPI0.DATA = sendBuffer[sendIndex];
      sendIndex++;
    } else { // All sent, disable interrupt
      SPI0.INTCTRL &= ~0x20;
    }
  }
  while ((SPI0.INTFLAGS & 0x80) != 0) { // data has arrived
    if (receiveIndex < 4) { // we have a place for it
      receiveBuffer[receiveIndex] = SPI0.DATA;
      receiveIndex++;
    } else { // Why is this here? just throw it out
      dummy = SPI0.DATA;
    }
  }
}
```

The SS pin interrupt ISR is similar in structure to the preceding example:

```
ISR(PORTE_PORT_vect) { // Interrupt vector for SS rising
  if (intflg.SLAVE_SS != 0) { // SS rising
    while ((SPI0.INTFLAGS & 0x80) != 0) {
      // there is a pending SPI interrupt, so do what it would
      // have done. It can only be data received at this point
      if (receiveIndex < 4) { // we have a place for it
        receiveBuffer[receiveIndex] = SPI0.DATA;
        receiveIndex++;
      } else { // Why is this here? just throw it out
        dummy = SPI0.DATA;
      }
    }
    // Values here are correct!
    // Our values are in receiveBuffer. Let's "process" them
    for (uint8_t i = 0; i < 4; i++) {
      sendBuffer[i] = receiveBuffer[i] + 1;
    }
    // Reset indices and enable data register empty interrupt
    receiveIndex = 0;
    sendIndex = 0;
    SPI0.CTRLA &= ~1; // turn off
    SPI0.INTCTRL |= 0x20;
    SPI0.CTRLA |= 1; // turn back on
    intflg.SLAVE_SS = 1; // reset pin interrupt flag
  }
}
```

In operation it can be seen that immediately after the SS interrupt return the first two bytes are sent to the transmitter. Because the buffer is kept full, there is no need for a delay between bytes.

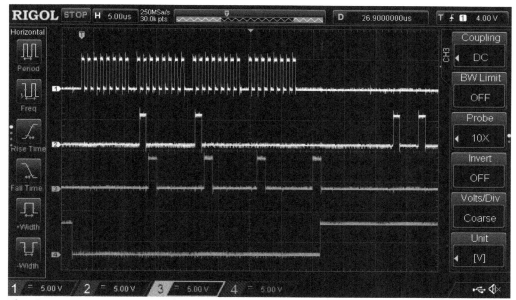

The bottom trace is SS. The top trace is SCK and shows the four bytes being transferred. The second trace from the top is high when a byte is being stored into SPI0.DATA. See how the first two bytes for the next transfer happen after SS goes high. The third trace from the top is high when a byte is being read from SPI0.DATA. This happens shortly (being the interrupt latency) after each byte is received.

The final example buffered program I need to qualify by saying that it is problematic. I apologize in advance for supplying an example program that cannot be relied upon. I've had it fail about once per hour in testing. This program is *SPI_SLAVE*. It is a buffered version of *SPI_SLAVE_UNBUFFERED*. It relies on the transmit buffer register instead of a variable to provide the additional byte of delay passing data through the slave SPI. It does not use DRIEF (perhaps that is part of the problem?) but relies on the availability to store in the transmit buffer by it being coordinated with bytes coming in the receiver.

The configuration code stores the initial two bytes to send in the transmit data buffer:

```
PORTMUX.TWISPIROUTEA |= PORTMUX_SPI0_ALT2_gc;
ddr.SLAVE_MISO = 1; // Config output pins
PORTE.PIN3CTRL = PORT_ISC_RISING_gc;
                    // Slave SS pin interrupts on rising edge
SPI0.CTRLA = 0x41; // Enable in slave mode, LSB first
SPI0.CTRLB = 0xc0; // Enable buffering
SPI0.INTCTRL = 0x80; // Interrupt when receive buffer has content
SPI0.DATA = 0; // First two bytes to send.
SPI0.DATA = 0;
```

The SPI ISR doesn't have to use a buffer variable but can load SPI0.DATA directly from what was just read from SPI0.DATA:

```
ISR(SPI0_INT_vect) { // A byte or more has come in
  do {
    // Keep last two bytes in
    inm2 = inm1;
    inm1 = SPI0.DATA;
    // data that goes out is that which just came in,
    // because of the hardware
    // transmit buffer already has a byte.
    SPI0.DATA = inm1;
  } while ((SPI0.INTFLAGS & 0x80) != 0); // Repeat until flag clears
}
```

The SS pin ISR stores the two bytes of "processed" data into SPI0.DATA for the next transfer:

```
ISR(PORTE_PORT_vect) { // Interrupt vector for SS rising
  if (intflg.SLAVE_SS != 0) { // SS rising
    while ((SPI0.INTFLAGS & 0x80) != 0) {
      // there is a pending SPI interrupt,
      // so do what it would have done
      //     SPI0.DATA = inm1;
      inm2 = inm1;
      inm1 = SPI0.DATA;
    }
    // Values here are correct!
    SPI0.CTRLA &= ~1; // Turn off SPI to reset
    // Our values are in inm2 (first received)
    // and inm1 (most recent received)
    // Let's return the product of the two bytes.
    uint16_t product = inm2 * inm1;
    inm1 = (uint8_t)(product & 0xff);
    inm2 = (uint8_t)(product >> 8);
    SPI0.CTRLA |= 1; // Turn SPI back on
    // We send the most significant byte first,
    // then the least significant
    SPI0.DATA =  inm2;
    SPI0.DATA = inm1;
    intflg.SLAVE_SS = 1; // reset pin interrupt flag
  }
}
```

If you count the number of bytes sent compared to that received, there appears to be two too many sent. These are in the transmit buffer when the SS pin goes high. By resetting the SPI, these bytes are cleared out before they would be sent.

CHAPTER TWENTY
USART

The Arduino Nano Every has four USARTs, two of which are hidden and must be enabled to use. While the transmit and receive data signals are brought out to board pins for all four USARTS, not all of the additional USART signals are brought out, which will limit potential functionality.

The USARTs are very similar to that found in the ATmega328P but there is some additional functionality. In brief:
- Half duplex operation (one-wire or RS485)
- Fractional baud rate generator
- Start of frame detection (only briefly discussed here)
- Can be used for infrared communication (not discussed further)
- Auto-baud (automatically set data rate, not discussed further)

Those features indicating "not discussed further" are simply beyond the scope of this book to cover in a reasonable number of pages. They also require special equipment to utilize.

These are in addition to features which are rarely used or not usable in the Arduino Uno/Nano:
- Synchronous operation
- Ability to run as an SPI master.
- Multiprocessor communication mode

These are useable in the Arduino Nano Every board and will be covered here.

The four USARTs are:
- USART0 - Not described in Arduino documentation, this uses D2 for TXD, D7 for RXD, A4 for XCK, and A5 for XDIR. This is the only USART with full signals directly available on the board.
- USART1 - This is device *Serial1* in the Arduino library and uses D1 for TXD, D0 for RXD, and has XCK available on D4. This uses alternate pins which must be set in the port multiplexer.
- USART2 - Not described in Arduino documentation, this uses D6 for TXD and D3 for RXD. Alternate pins are used which must be set in the port multiplexer.
- USART3 - Connects to the USB interface and is device *Serial* in the Arduino library. Signals not brought out on the board.

The port multiplexer must be changed from its default to use USART1, USART2, or USART3. This can be accomplished with the instruction:

```
PORTMUX.USARTROUTEA = PORTMUX_USART1_ALT1_gc |
PORTMUX_USART2_ALT1_gc |
PORTMUX_USART3_ALT1_gc;
```

Using device *Serial* or *Serial1* in the Arduino library will set the port multiplex for USART3 or USART1 respectively. It will also take over the RXC and DRE interrupt vectors for the USART.

The XCK pin (accessible for USART0 and USART1) is the clock in/out pin for synchronous operation or as SCK out when used as an SPI master. The XDIR pin (accessible only for USART0 without using the Event System) is direction control output for RS-485 operation. This means that if we want additional SPI master interfaces we can use USART0 and/or USART1 while still having USART3 for USB connectivity to a computer and USART2 for general asynchronous serial communication. While the XDIR pin is convenient for RS-485 operation, it isn't necessary.

Let's run through the USART registers first before looking at applications. The "n" in the register names need to be replaced with the USART number, 0 through 3.

Status Register USARTn.STATUS

Bit	7	6	5	4	3	2	1	0
Function	RXCIF	TXCIF	DREIF	RXSIF	ISFIF		BDF	WFB

RXCIF — USART receive complete flag. Set to 1 if there is unread data and cleared when it is empty. The RXDATA register needs to be read to clear the flag. TXCIF — USART transmit complete flag. Set to 1 when the transmitter is empty and shifting out is complete. Documentation claims automatically cleared when the interrupt routine USARTn_TXC is entered, however I've found that not to be the case. It can be cleared by writing a "1" to it. DREIF — USART data register empty flag. Set to 1 when the transmit buffer is empty and to 0 when it contains data not yet transferred to the transmit shift register. Any USARTn_DRE interrupt routine must either store into TXDATA or disable the interrupt. RXSIF flag is used by the start of frame detection and the ISFIF, BDF, and WFB flags are used by auto-baud.

Control A Register USARTn.CTRLA

Bit	7	6	5	4	3	2	1	0
Function	RXCIE	TXCIE	DREIE	RXSIE	LBME	ABEIE	RS485-1	RS485-0

The top four bits are interrupt enables. RXCIE enables the RXC interrupt when RXCIF is set. TXCIE enables the TXC interrupt when TXCIF is set. DREIE enables the DRE interrupt when DREIF is set. RXSIE enables the RXC interrupt when RXSIF is set.

LBME enables loop back mode. The TXD pin is internally connected to the USART receiver and the RXD pin is disabled. This basically wires the part for 1-wire operation where the TXD pin both transmits and receives. ABEIE is the interrupt enable for auto-baud error, ISFIF, and will cause an RXC interrupt.

RS485 is for half-duplex, RS485 mode of operation. RS485-0 raises XDIR high one clock cycle before the start of transmission and lowers it at the end of transmission. This is used to control an RS-485 interface IC direction. RS485-1 sets the TXD pin to output one clock cycle before transmission and sets it back to input at the end of transmission. When combined with the 1-wire operation, this frees up the RXD pin for other uses.

Control B Register USARTn.CTRLB

Bit	7	6	5	4	3	2	1	0
Function	RXEN	TXEN		SFDEN	ODME	RXMODE		MPCM

RXEN enables the receiver. TXEN enables the transmitter. If the transmitter is turned off while there is still data in the transmit buffer or shift register, turn off is delayed until operations complete. Also, when the transmitter is enabled, it drives the TX pin. When disabled it becomes a GPIO input pin even if it were originally configured as an output. The direction of the TX pin must be changed to output when enabling the transmitter.

SFDEN enables the start of frame detector. This will set the RXSIF flag and potentially cause the RXC interrupt at the start of a frame. This allows waking up the system from idle or standby sleep modes when a byte starts arriving.

ODME disables the transmitter pullup transistor, putting it in "open drain" mode. This is used for 1-wire operation where we want to "or" all the transmitters together. Contrast this with RS485-1 which uses the pullup transistor and can cause a short if two devices drive the signal simultaneously.

RXMODE sets the receiver mode. It should normally be 0. A value of 1 doubles the transmission speed by halving the number of clocks per bit from 16 to 8. The other two values are used by auto-baud mode.

MPCM enables multi-processor communication mode. In this mode there are address and data frames, the type indicated by the most significant data bit. Usually 9 data bits are used and the 9th bit indicates the frame is an address frame when 1. The receiving microcontrollers see only the address frames when MPCM is set, and look for an address byte that matches their predetermined address. An addressed microcontroller then turns off the MPCM bit and receives the following data frames while the unaddressed microcontrollers will not see the data frames.

Control C Register USARTn.CTRLC

Bit	7	6	5	4	3	2	1	0
Not SPI	CMODE		PMODE		SBMODE	CHSIZE		
SPI	1	1				UDORD	UCPHA	

The bits in this register take on different uses depending on if the USART is in master SPI mode or not. The CMODE field is in common:

Value	Name	Description
0	USART_CMODE_ASYNCHRONOUS_gc	Asynchronous USART mode
1	USART_CMODE_SYNCHRONOUS_gc	Synchronous USART mode
2	USART_CMODE_IRCOM_gc	Infrared mode
3	USART_CMODE_MSPI_gc	SPI master mode

The PMODE bits set the party generation and expected received parity. A value of 0 disables parity. A value of 2 (USART_PMODE_EVEN_gc) adds an even parity bit and a value of 3 (USART_PMODE_ODD_gc) adds an odd parity bit. SBMODE of 1 adds a second stop bit to the transmitted data.

CHSIZE sets the character size according to the following table:

Value	Name	Description
0	USART_CHSIZE_5BIT_gc	5 data bits
1	USART_CHSIZE_6BIT_gc	6 data bits
2	USART_CHSIZE_7BIT_gc	7 data bits
3	USART_CHSIZE_8BIT_gc	8 data bits
6	USART_CHSIZE_9BITL_gc	9 data bits, low byte first
7	USART_CHSIZE_9BITH_gc	9 data bits, high byte first

In master SPI mode, the UDORD value of 1 will transmit LSB first, otherwise the MSB is transmitted first. UCPHA sets the clock phase like the conventional CPHA bit in the SPI module. The clock polarity is positive. It can be made negative by setting the INVEN bit in the Pin Control register for the pin.

Baud Register USARTn.BAUD (16-bit register)
This 16-bit register sets the clock divider. This is a fractional divider in that the register value is shifted right 6 bits (divided by 64) to get the division factor. The value needed depends on the desired data rate, *BAUD*, the clock frequency, *FREQ*,

and the number of samples per bit, S. In normal asynchronous mode S=16, while in double speed mode S=8, and in synchronous modes (USART or SPI) S=2. The value for the register is (64*FREQ)/(S*BAUD). The following statement will set the USART0 baud register at 9600 bps in asynchronous mode:
```
USART0.BAUD = (4*F_CPU)/9600;
```
while to set 19200 bps in synchronous mode would use the statement:
```
USART0.BAUD = ((32*F_CPU)/19200)&0xffc0;
```

Note that the value in this register must be at least 64, corresponding to a division factor of 1. The fractional bits (bits 0 through 5) are should be zero in synchronous mode. The maximum value is 65535 which limits the minimum asynchronous data rate to 1200bps (standard rate) with a 16MHz clock or 2400bps with a 20MHz clock. If one needs to run slower then a slower clock speed must be selected. See Clocks, Resets, Lock and Fuse Bits (page 123).

For a more accurate rate in asynchronous operation, the frequency error calibration factor can be used when setting the BAUD register. From the data sheet:
```
int8_t sigrow_val = SIGROW.OSC16ERR5V;
                // use OSC20ERR5V for 20MHz clock
int32_t baud_reg_val = (4*F_CPU)/9600;  // 9600bps
baud_reg_val *= (1024 + sigrow_val);
baud_reg_val /= 1024;
USART0.BAUD = (int16_t) baud_reg_val;
```

Receiver Data Register USARTn.RXDATA (16-bit), RXDATAL, RXDATAH (8-bit)

Bit	7	6	5	4	3	2	1	0
RXDATAH	RXCIF	BUFOVF				FERR	PERR	DATA8
RXDATAL	DATA7	DATA6	DATA5	DATA4	DATA3	DATA2	DATA1	DATA0

The receiver data register also has receiver error flags and a mirror of the RXCIF flag. Applications not caring about the error flags and using 8 or fewer data bits can just read the RXDATAL register. If the error flags need to be read, they must be read before RXDATAL. Since the C++ compiler will always read the low byte of a 16-bit word first, reading as a word, RXDATA, is not possible. But there is an exception. When using 9 data bits and specifying 9BITL in the CHSIZE field of CTRLC, the low order byte must be read first, and RXDATA can be read. Only use 9BITH if it is intended to only access one byte at a time.

The error flags are valid only for the current received character frame and include BUFOVF for buffer overflow, FERR for frame error, and PERR for parity error.

Transmitter Data Register USARTn.TXDATA (16-bit), TXDATAL, TXDATAH (8-bit)

Bit	7	6	5	4	3	2	1	0
TXDATAH								DATA8
TXDATAL	DATA7	DATA6	DATA5	DATA4	DATA3	DATA2	DATA1	DATA0

When there are fewer than 9 data bits, only TXDATAL should be written. When there are 9 data bits, the same rules about ordering RXDATA apply here — for writing the whole word use CHSIZE 9BITL. If 9BITH is selected the high byte TXDATAH must be written before the low byte TXDATAL.

There are other registers used for auto-baud and infrared that won't be covered here.

Normal Asynchronous Operation Example

In most of these examples we will be communicating between USART0 and USART1. Both USARTs are configured to use ISRs for transmitting and receiving, and the ISRs read from and write to circular buffers (FIFOs). Code in the loop function keep the data flowing.

Normal Asynchronous Operation

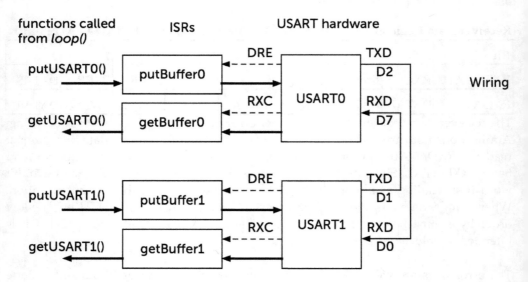

The program is *USART_ASYNC*. D1 (labeled TX) needs to be connected to D7 and D0 (labeled RX) needs to be connected to D2. The constant BAUDRATE sets the baud rate and the constant SPREAD sets the frame rate in microseconds. If it is less than the size of the frame then data is transmitted continuously. Spreading it out makes operation easier to see on an oscilloscope. The code for the ISRs and the buffer management is just a slightly modified version of that for the ATmega328P, as discussed in *Far Inside The Arduino*, and won't be discussed here. The port multiplexer must be set up as well as the transmitter pins (D1 and D2) set for output. The USARTs are initialized with the same values, as shown here for USART0:

```
ddr.digital_2 = 1; // Set TX pins as outputs and drive them high.
port.digital_2 = 1;
USART0.CTRLC = USART_CHSIZE_8BIT_gc; // 8 bits, no parity 1 stop bit
USART0.BAUD = (4 * F_CPU) / BAUDRATE;
USART0.CTRLB = 0xc0; // RXEN and TXEN
USART0.CTRLA = 0x80; // RXCIE. DREIE turned on when
                     // there is something to send
```

Global interrupts should be disabled during configuration.

The oscilloscope capture with USART0 TXD on the top and RXD on the bottom, 9600 baud with SPREAD of 2500:

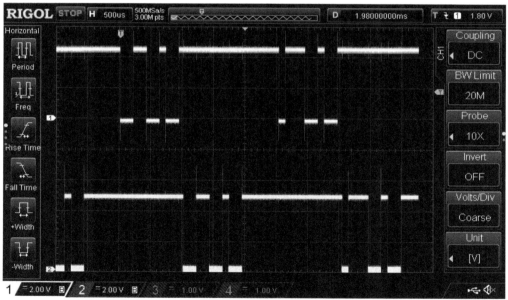

Synchronous Operation Example

Synchronous operation requires that XCK of the USARTs be connected together. That would be pins A4 and D4. USART0 will be used as the clock source, so its XCK pin is configured as an output. USART1 then uses the XCK signal to clock its shift register.

Normal Synchronous Operation

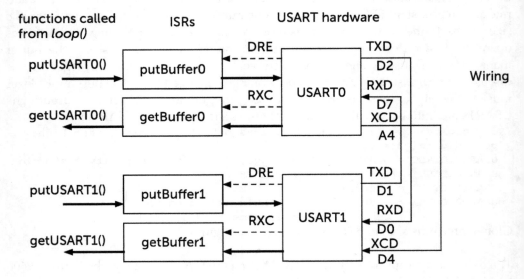

functions called from *loop()* | ISRs | USART hardware | Wiring

Other functions: isFulln() and isEmptyn() for put and get, respectively

The example program is *USART_SYNC*. Configuration for USART0 is:
```
ddr.digital_2 = 1; // Set TX pins as outputs and drive them high.
port.digital_2 = 1;
ddr.analog_4 = 1; // XCK output on USART0 (master)
// Configure USART0
USART0.CTRLC = USART_CMODE_SYNCHRONOUS_gc | USART_CHSIZE_8BIT_gc;
        // 8 bits, no parity 1 stop bit, synchronous mode
USART0.BAUD = (32 * F_CPU) / BAUDRATE; // Not needed for USART1!
USART0.CTRLB = 0xc0; // RXEN and TXEN
USART0.CTRLA = 0x80; // RXCIE. DREIE turned on when
                     // there is something to send
```
Global interrupts should be disabled during configuration.

The oscilloscope capture with the added bottom trace showing XCD. Configuration is 100,000 baud with SPREAD of 200:

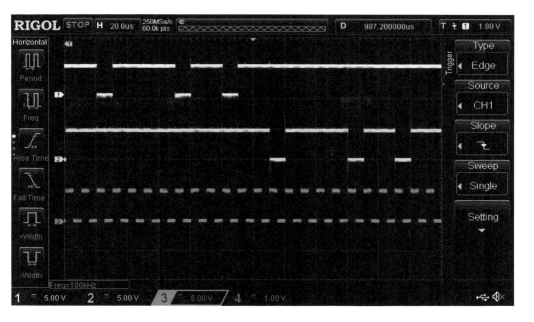

Half Duplex (1-wire) Operation Example

When configured for 1-wire operation, only the TX pins are used as they are internally connected to the receivers. The pins have pull-ups enabled and run in open drain mode.

Half Duplex (1 Wire) Asynchronous Operation

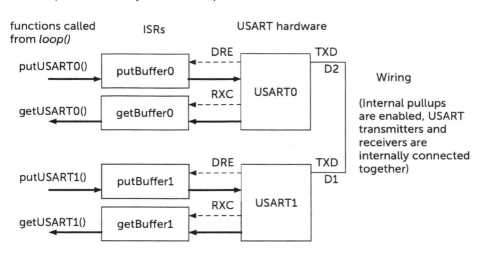

Other functions: isFulln() and isEmptyn() for put and get, respectively

The example program, *USART_1WIRE*, send a block of data (5 bytes in this case) from USART0 to USART1 and then another block of data from USART1 to USART0. Normally a software protocol would be necessary to prevent two transmitters attempting to operate simultaneously, but the text program having only a single execution thread prevents this. Local echo is verified against send data. If we didn't want the local echo then it would be necessary to turn off the receiver while transmitting. A small delay is added for better oscilloscope display. The setup code for USART0 is:

```
PORTA.PINOCTRL |= 1 << PORT_PULLUPEN_bp; // Enable pullup D2
USART0.CTRLC = USART_CHSIZE_8BIT_gc; // 8 bits, no parity 1 stop bit
USART0.BAUD = (4 * F_CPU) / BAUDRATE;
USART0.CTRLB = 0xc8; // RXEN TXEN ODME
USART0.CTRLA = 0x88; // RXCIE, LBME. DREIE turned on when
                     // there is something to send
```

Global interrupts should be disabled during configuration.

The oscilloscope trace alternates the data in each direction:

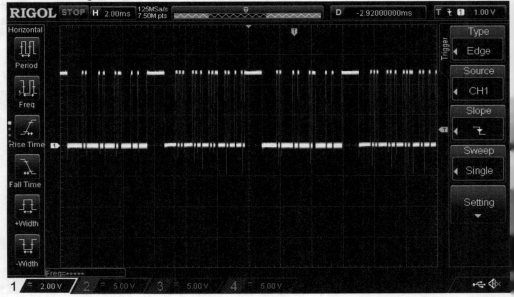

RS-485 Operation Example

Operation in RS-485 mode is similar to the 1-wire operation, but uses line drivers and differential signaling to operate over long distances at high speed. Instead of setting ODME and LBME to 1, RS485-0 is set to 1, enabling the use of the XDIR pin to control the direction of the line driver. Loopback mode can be used as well to free up the RXD pin for other use.

The example program *USART_RS485* is is identical to the *USART_1WIRE* program but for the configuration difference and the elimination of reading loopback data. There is the problem of XDIR for USART1 not being accessible on the Nano Every board. This was solved by using the Event System to route port pin PC7, which is XDIR for USART1, to EVBOUTB, which is D5 on the Nano Every board. Configuration code for USART1 is:

```
ddr.digital_5 = 1; // XDIR output
ddr.digital_1 = 1; // TX output

USART1.CTRLC = USART_CHSIZE_8BIT_gc; // 8 bits, no parity 1 stop bit
USART1.BAUD = (4 * F_CPU) / BAUDRATE;
USART1.CTRLB = 0xc0; // RXEN  TXEN
USART1.CTRLA = 0x81; // RXCIE, RS232. DREIE turned on when
                     // there is something to send

// XDIR is on PC7, route it to D5
VPORTC.DIR |= 1<<7;
EVSYS.CHANNEL2 = EVSYS_GENERATOR_PORT0_PIN7_gc;
EVSYS.USEREVOUTB = EVSYS_CHANNEL_CHANNEL2_gc;
```

The oscilloscope trace shows USART0 TXD, the differential line drive signal A-B, A, and B, and the USART1 RXD. The differential signal also shows the return data from USART1 to USART0.

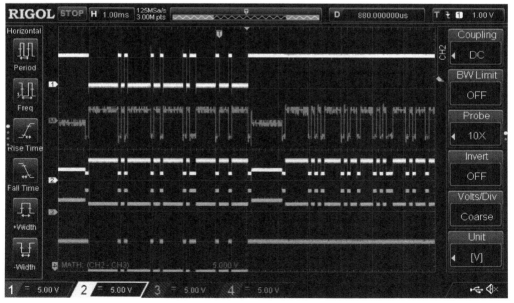

SPI Operation Example

To demonstrate SPI operation, the example program *USART_AS_MSPI* combines a USART0 running in master SPI mode with the slave SPI example in example *SPI_SLAVE_BUFFERED*. The USART0 code is similar to that used for the SPI in the *SPI_MASTER* example.There are three interrupts available. Remember that sending and receiving occur simultaneously. If we use DRE interrupt it will indicate that the transmitter buffer is empty, but that doesn't mean that a byte has been received. If we use the TXC interrupt then the byte we wrote to TXDATAL has been shifted out, so there must be a byte shifted in. The code uses this single interrupt vector if *TWOISRVERSION* is not defined. As in *SPI_MASTER,* there is a small break between the transmission of each byte. We can get rid of the break by defining *TWOISRVERSION*. Then there will be an RXC interrupt as well as a TXC interrupt. The RXC interrupt occurs earlier, allowing writing to TXDATAL earlier, causing the break to disappear. If we use just the RXC interrupt, it occurs before the final SCK clock pulse is finished, and SS would go high too soon. So SS is raised in the TXC ISR. The operation looks like:

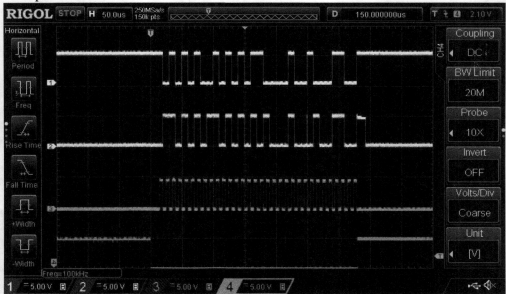

showing MOSI, MISO, SCK, and SS from top to bottom. This is transferring four bytes at 100kHz.

Setup code for the USART:

```
ddr.MASTER_MOSI = 1;
ddr.MASTER_SS = 1;
port.MASTER_SS = 1;
ddr.MASTER_SCK = 1;
USART0.CTRLC = USART_CMODE_MSPI_gc | 4; // MSPI mode, LSB first
USART0.BAUD = (32 * F_CPU) / BAUDRATE;
USART0.CTRLB = 0xc0; // RXEN and TXEN
#ifdef TWOISRVERSION
USART0.CTRLA = 0xC0; // RXCIE, TXCIE
#else
USART0.CTRLA = 0x40; // TXCIE
#endif
```

Variable declarations are:

```
uint8_t masterOutData[4] = {0x55, 0xaa, 0x21, 0x31};
uint8_t masterInData[4] = {0, 0, 0, 0};
volatile uint8_t masterIndex;
```

The *masterIndex* variable starts at zero and counts up to four with each byte transferred. This code in the loop function starts the first transfer and then waits for all four bytes to be transferred:

```
port.MASTER_SS = 0;
masterIndex = 0;
USART0.TXDATAL = masterOutData[0]; // Start things running
while (masterIndex < 4) ; // wait until it completes
```

The pair of ISRs for the TWOISRVERSION are:

```
ISR(USART0_RXC_vect) { // A byte has come in (and one has gone out)
  masterInData[masterIndex++] = USART0.RXDATAL;
  if (masterIndex < 4) { // send another byte out
    USART0.TXDATAL = masterOutData[masterIndex];
  }
}

ISR(USART0_TXC_vect) { // use this to turn off SS
  port.MASTER_SS = 1;
  USART0.STATUS |= 0x40; // clear the flag
}
```

CHAPTER TWENTY-ONE
TWI/I2C

In the ATmega4809 the TWI interface is split into two independent parts, one for the master and one for the slave. The Arduino Nano Every board ties the master and slave pins together and the library makes the assumption both master and slave would not be used at the same time.

I don't recommend writing code to access the TWI interface directly because it is complicated and there basically is little performance to be gained. The Arduino Library for the Nano Every uses a modified version of the Microchip library, which is well written and much more efficient of memory than the ATmega328P code in the Arduino library. Use the files *twi.h* and *twi.c* directly without the rest of the Wire library. It does not contain any data buffers, which saves RAM memory. You must supply any necessary buffers in your code.

I did find some patches that I deem necessary. The library intentionally does not allow using the master and slave TWI simultaneously. This is easily fixed. Also the new bi-directional transfer function *TWI_MasterWriteRead* is documented to return an error/success value but was modified so that it was only doing a read it would return the number of bytes read. I changed that back to the original return value.

All the master transfer functions are blocking. For non-blocking operation it would be easy to modify the code. I haven't done so but here are some quick instructions. Find the line commented "Arduino requires blocking function" in *TWI_MasterWriteRead*. If you change the function to return at that point it becomes non-blocking. To determine when the operation completes, make the variable *master_result* global and volatile. If the command hasn't finished, it will read TWI_RESULT_UNKNOWN, which is the value 0. It is set with the return status, of type TWIM_RESULT_t, when the command finishes.

Operation of the TWI Master
The necessary functions are:
`void TWI_MasterInit(uint32_t frequency)`
This must be called to initialize the TWI master module. The value for *frequency* should normally be 100000L. It replaces twi_init(), which defaulted to 100kHz clock speed.

```
uint8_t TWI_MasterWrite(uint8_t slave_address,
                        uint8_t *write_data,
                        uint8_t bytes_to_write,
                        uint8_t send_stop)
```

This function is used to write data to a slave device. It replaces twi_writeTo(), but always blocks. This could be considered important because there is no buffering and by blocking it doesn't matter since the write buffer cannot be overwritten before being sent. It returns zero if successful or non-zero if an error occurs.

```
uint8_t TWI_MasterRead(uint8_t slave_address,
                       uint8_t* read_data,
                       uint8_t bytes_to_read,
                       uint8_t send_stop)
```

This function is used to read data from a slave device. It replaces twi_readFrom(). Again there is no buffering in the new function. It is now possible to read 0 bytes in order to signal a stop without actually reading. It returns the number of bytes read, which unless there is an error will be the same as *bytes_to_read*.

```
uint8_t TWI_MasterWriteRead(uint8_t slave_address,
                            uint8_t *write_data,
                            uint8_t bytes_to_write,
                            uint8_t bytes_to_read,
                            uint8_t send_stop)
```

This function is new and both writes and then reads. It is called by TWI_MasterWrite and TWI_MasterRead, so all the work is actually done here. After modification it returns non-zero, an error code, if an error occurs.

TWI Master Example

The provided example of operation as a TWI master, *zs042_twi*, is the Arduino Nano Every version of the program provided for the Arduino Uno in *Far Inside The Arduino*. This uses the common ZS-042 board which has a DS3231 real-time clock and an Atmel 24C32 4096x8 EEPROM. The example program exercises both the clock and the EEPROM.

Operation of the TWI Slave

Slave operation is done through callback functions after initialization.
```
void TWI_SlaveInit(uint8_t address);
```
After modification of the source, it is possible to initialize both the master and slave simultaneously. The argument to TWI_SlaveInit is the slave's address.

```
void TWI_attachSlaveRxEvent(void (*function)(int),
                            uint8_t *read_data,
                            uint8_t bytes_to_read );
```

This function is called to set up the callback function for receiving data as a slave. Because there is no buffer in the TWI driver code, this function also specifies the address of the buffer to put the read data and the maximum number of bytes that can be received, usually the size of *read_data*. The callback function is called when data has been received, with the argument being the actual number of bytes received.

```
void TWI_attachSlaveTxEvent(uint8_t (*function)(void),
                            uint8_t *write_data );
```
This function is called to set up the callback function transmitting data as a slave. Because there is no buffer in the TWI driver code, this function also specifies the address of the buffer containing the data to send. The callback function is called prior to transmitting the data which allows changing the data prior to sending. The callback function returns the number of bytes to transmit.

TWI Slave Example

While the example programs provided in the Arduino IDE require two boards to demonstrate slave operation, either running *master_reader* and *slave_sender*, or *master_writer* and *slave_receiver*, the single example program here, *TWI_MASTER_SLAVE* combines all four functions into a single program by using the TWI master module and TWI slave module simultaneously. This does require the modified *twi.c* that is provided.

Declarations are needed for the callback functions and the slave data buffers, as well as the slave address:
```
#define SLAVE_ADDR 8
void receiveEvent(int);
uint8_t requestEvent(void);
uint8_t slaveReadBuf[8];
uint8_t slaveWriteBuf[] = "Hello ";
```

The *setup* function initializes both the master and slave TWI modules. It then specifies the callback functions for the slave:
```
TWI_MasterInit(100000L);
TWI_SlaveInit(SLAVE_ADDR); // slave address SLAVE_ADDR
TWI_attachSlaveRxEvent(receiveEvent,
                       slaveReadBuf,
                       sizeof(slaveReadBuf));
TWI_attachSlaveTxEvent(requestEvent,
                       slaveWriteBuf);
```

The *loop* function does the data transfers for the master:

```
uint8_t data[6] = "x is "; // 5 characters, data[5] is counter
uint8_t dataIn[8];
void loop()
{
  // Send 6 bytes to slave address SLAVE_ADDR
  TWI_MasterWrite(SLAVE_ADDR, data, 6, true);
  data[5]++; // Next write will be different.
  // request 6 bytes from slave device SLAVE_ADDR
  TWI_MasterRead(SLAVE_ADDR, dataIn, 6, true);
  Serial.print((char *)dataIn);
  delay(500);
}
```

The data transfers for the slave are done entirely in callback functions from the TWI ISR:

```
// function that executes whenever data is received from master
void receiveEvent(int howMany) {
  int charCount = howMany - 1;
  uint8_t *buf = slaveReadBuf;
  while (charCount-- > 0) Serial.print((char)*buf++);
  Serial.println(*buf);
}
```

```
// function that executes whenever data is requested by master
uint8_t requestEvent() {
  return 6; // respond with message of 6 bytes
            // as expected by master
}
```

CHAPTER TWENTY-TWO
Configurable Custom Logic

Configurable Custom Logic is basically an attempt to put a small FPGA into the microcontroller. It might be useful for eliminating the need for small amounts of logic circuits external to the microcontroller when the microcontroller does not offer sufficient performance to process the signals. As an overview:

- There are four channels, or lookup tables (LUTs).
- Each LUT performs any combinatorial logic function of three inputs.
- Each input can come from many sources including digital input pins, events, the output of this or another LUT, or an internal peripheral.
- The output of the logic function can optionally go through a synchronizer to the LUT clock domain or both the synchronizer and a filter for noise immunity.
- The output of the synchronizer/filter can optionally go through an edge detector.
- The outputs from an even/odd pair of LUTs can optionally go into one of several types of flip-flop or latches, referred to as the sequencer, to become the even LUT output.
- The final output of a LUT can go to output pins and the Event System.

All of this is configured via register settings. Rather than list all the registers at once, this chapter will work its way through the signal flow through a LUT and look at the appropriate register fields as we progress.

There is a single CCL control register:
Control A Register CCL.CTRLA

Bit	7	6	5	4	3	2	1	0
Function		RUNSTBY						ENABLE

RUNSTBY allows the CLK_PER (system) clock to be supplied when in standby sleep mode. The ENABLE bit enables the CCL. This bit must be 1 to use the CCL.

Each LUT also has an enable bit. The LUT cannot be configured unless this bit is 0. The enable bit is the least significant bit of the LUT's Control A register. Initially the LUTs are disabled.

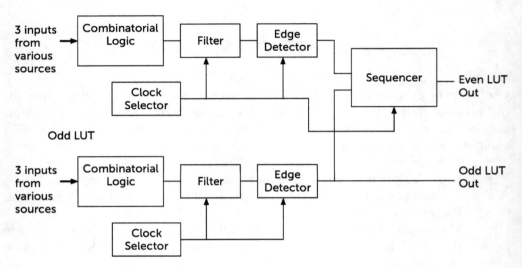

Configuring the Combinatorial Logic

The combinatorial logic in a LUT has three inputs, each selected from a number of sources, and can create a specific output by using the three inputs to index and select a bit in the TRUTH register.

CCL -- Combinatorial Logic

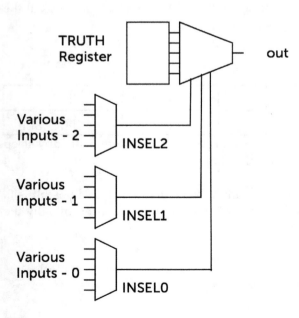

The three INSEL values and the TRUTH register value are set from three registers.

LUT n Control B Register CCL.LUTnCTRLB

Bit	7	6	5	4	3	2	1	0
Function	INSEL1				INSEL0			

Each input has slightly different signal choices.

INSEL0

Value	Constant	Description
0	CCL_INSEL0_MASK_gc	Constant value 0
1	CCL_INSEL0_FEEDBACK_gc	Output of this LUNs sequencer
2	CCL_INSEL0_LINK_gc	Output of LUT(n+1)
3	CCL_INSEL0_EVENTA_gc	Event System User A
4	CCL_INSEL0_EVENTB_gc	Event System User B
5	CCL_INSEL0_IO_gc	GPIO Pin (see below)
6	CCL_INSEL0_AC0_gc	Analog Comparator Output
8	CCL_INSEL0_USART0_gc	USART0 TXD
9	CCL_INSEL0_SPI0_gc	SPI MOSI
10	CCL_INSEL0_TCA0_gc	TCA0 WO0
12	CCL_INSEL0_TCB0_gc	TCB0 WO

INSEL1

Value	Constant	Description
0	CCL_INSEL1_MASK_gc	Constant value 0
1	CCL_INSEL1_FEEDBACK_gc	Output of this LUNs sequencer
2	CCL_INSEL1_LINK_gc	Output of LUT(n+1)
3	CCL_INSEL1_EVENTA_gc	Event System User A
4	CCL_INSEL1_EVENTB_gc	Event System User B
5	CCL_INSEL1_IO_gc	GPIO Pin (see below)
6	CCL_INSEL1_AC0_gc	Analog Comparator Output
8	CCL_INSEL1_USART1_gc	USART1 TXD
9	CCL_INSEL1_SPI0_gc	SPI MOSI
10	CCL_INSEL1_TCA0_gc	TCA0 WO1
12	CCL_INSEL1_TCB1_gc	TCB1 WO

LUT n Control C Register CCL.LUTnCTRLC

Bit	7	6	5	4	3	2	1	0
Function					INSEL2			

INSEL2

Value	Constant	Description
0	CCL_INSEL2_MASK_gc	Constant value 0
1	CCL_INSEL2_FEEDBACK_gc	Output of this LUNs sequencer
2	CCL_INSEL2_LINK_gc	Output of LUT(n+1)
3	CCL_INSEL2_EVENTA_gc	Event System User A
4	CCL_INSEL2_EVENTB_gc	Event System User B
5	CCL_INSEL2_IO_gc	GPIO Pin (see below)
6	CCL_INSEL2_AC0_gc	Analog Comparator Output
8	CCL_INSEL2_USART2_gc	USART2 TXD
9	CCL_INSEL2_SPI0_gc	SPI SCK
10	CCL_INSEL2_TCA0_gc	TCA0 WO2
12	CCL_INSEL2_TCB2_gc	TCB2 WO

Each of the four LUTs has two event users, A and B, for eight total. The GPIO pin assignments on the Arduino Nano Every for each input and the output of each LUT are conveniently listed in this table. Those signals that aren't brought out to board pins can still be accessed in the microcontroller by their port location:

GPIO connections

LUT	Input 0	Input 1	Input 2	Output
LUT0	D2	D7	A4	A5
LUT1	PC0	PC1	PC2	PC3
LUT2	A3	A2	A1	A0
LUT3	PF0	PF1	A4	A5

Note that Input 2 for LUT0 and LUT3 are connected together on the Arduino Nano Every board, as are the outputs for LUT0 and LUT3.

LUT n Truth Table Register CCL.TRUTHn

Bit	7	6	5	4	3	2	1	0
Function	I2 I1 I0	I2 I1 I0'	I2 I1' I0	I2 I1' I0'	I2' I1 I0	I2' I1 I0'	I2' I1' I0	I2' I1' I0'

The function description for the truth table shows the combination of the three inputs that select the value in the bit. The selected bit will be the output of the combinatorial logic.

For instance, the function (I0 + I1)*I2 is true only for inputs I2 I1 I0, I2 I1 I0' and I2 I1' I0, so would be in the truth table as the value 0xE0.

Configuring the Clock, Filter, and Edge Detector

The clock is used by the filter, edge detector, and the sequencer. All but the sequencer are configured in a single register:

LUT n Control A Register CCL.LUTnCTRLA

Bit	7	6	5	4	3	2	1	0
Function	EDGEDET	OUTEN	FILTSEL		CLKSRC			ENABLE

The ENABLE bit enables the LUT. None of the other bits in this register or any related register to the LUT can be altered if this bit is 1.The CLKSRC bits select the clock source. The choices are:

Value	Constant	Description
0	CCL_CLKSRC_CLKPER_gc	System clock
1	CCL_CLKSRC_IN2_gc	LUT input 2
4	CCL_CLKSRC_OSC20M_gc	16/20Mhz oscillator
5	CCL_CLKSRC_OSCULP32K_gc	32.768kHz oscillator
6	CCL_CLKSRC_OSCULP1K_gc	1.024 kHz (32k divided by 32)

Unless a system clock divider is used or RUNSTBY=1, choice 0 and 4 will be the same.

FILTSEL selects a filter to use. CCL_FILTSEL_DISABLE_gc (value 0) doesn't us any filter and the output of the combinatorial logic goes directly to the edge detector. CCL_FILTSEL_SYNC_gc (value 1) adds a synchronizer to synchronize the combinatorial logic output to the LUT clock domain. It adds a two clock period delay. CCL_FILTSEL_FILTER_gc both synchronizes and low pass filters the signal. The signal must be high for two clock periods to get a high output. It inserts a total of four clock periods of delay.

When EDGEDET is 1, the edge detector is used and will produce a one LUT clock period long pulse on the rising edge of the (potentially) filtered signal. OUTEN enables the output pin for the LUT, discussed later.

Configuring the Sequencer (Flip-Flop)

There is one sequencer for each pair of LUTs. LUT0 and LUT1 make the pair for Sequencer 0, while LUT2 and LUT3 make the pair for Sequencer 1. The clock for the sequencer is the clock for the even LUT. A sequencer is cleared (output forced to 0) by disabling the even LUT. The sequencer used is selected in one of the following two registers (n=0, 1):

Sequencer Control n Register CCL.SEQCTRLn

Bit	7	6	5	4	3	2	1	0
Function					SEQSEL			

The values, sequencer type, and connections are:

Value	Constant	Type	Even LUT Input	Odd LUT input
0	CCL_SEQSELn_DISABLE_gc	Disabled		
1	CCL_SEQSELn_DFF_gc	D flip-flop	D - data	G - enable
2	CCL_SEQSELn_JK_gc	JK flip-flop	J - set	K - clear
3	CCL_SEQSELn_LATCH_gc	D latch	D - data	G - load
4	CCL_SEQSELn_RS_gc	RS latch	S - set	R - clear

The inputs are the outputs of the edge detectors. All flip-flop types are clocked by the even LUT clock. The output of the even LUT is the sequencer output if the LUT is enabled. If it is disabled it is the output of the even LUT edge detector.

Configuring the Output

The outputs of the LUTs can go back as inputs to the LUTs, drive an GPIO pin, act as an Event Generator, and/or trigger an interrupt. They can connect to the LUTs input with CCL_INSELn_FEEDBACK_gc,or to the next lower numbered (where 3 is next lower than 0) LUTs input with CCL_INSEL0_LINK_gc. The OUTEN bit enables driving the GPIO pin listed in the GPIO connections table, above. OUTEN=1 overrides any setting of the GPIO pin.

As an event generator the generator value is EVSYS_GENERATOR_CCL_LUTn_gc.

All four LUTs can trigger a single interrupt, CCL_CCL. There are two registers used.

Interrupt Control 0 Register CCL.INTCTRL0

Bit	7	6	5	4	3	2	1	0
Function	INTMODE3		INTMODE2		INTMODE1		INTMODE0	

Sets the interrupt sense condition that triggers the interrupt for each of the four LUTs. The values are 0 to disable, 1 for rising edge, 2 for falling edge, and 3 for both edges.

Interrupt Flags Register CCL.INTFLAGS

Bit	7	6	5	4	3	2	1	0
Function					INT3	INT2	INT1	INT0

The corresponding flag bit is set when the interrupt sense condition occurs on the LUT. A flag bit must be cleared by writing a "1" to it.

Examples of Use

The example program *CCL* is simple in that it only uses the combinatorial logic in a LUT, and not the additional features or the sequencer. It uses LUT1, for which the inputs and output are not presented on the Arduino Nano Every board. That won't stop us from using it, and will demonstrate that sometimes you don't really need physical pins on the board. The LUT uses port C bits 0 through 2 for inputs and bit 3 for the output. The direction of all four are set to output. We can still read the voltage level on the (inaccessible) pins.

The input pattern 1 0 0 (PC2 high and PC1 and PC0 low) will make the output on PC3 go high and will also cause an interrupt. The ISR prints a message. The program loop goes through all combinations of inputs, printing the input value and the output value for each case.

The CCL configuration in setup is:
```
VPORTC.DIR |= 0x0f; // Make them all output pins
CCL.LUT1CTRLB = CCL_INSEL0_IO_gc | CCL_INSEL1_IO_gc;
CCL.LUT1CTRLC = CCL_INSEL2_IO_gc;
CCL.TRUTH1 = 0x10; // Only high output for input 1 0 0
CCL.LUT1CTRLA = CCL_OUTEN_bm | CCL_ENABLE_bm;
CCL.INTCTRL0 = 1 << 2; // Rising edge interrupt
CCL.CTRLA = 1; // Enable the CCL
```

The ISR is:

```
ISR(CCL_CCL_vect) {
  Serial.println("Triggered!");
  CCL.INTFLAGS = 0x2;
}
```

Finally, the program loop is:

```
void loop() {
  static uint8_t counter;
  VPORTC.OUT = (VPORTC.OUT & 0xf0) | counter;
  Serial.print("In: ");
  Serial.print(counter, BIN);
  Serial.print(" Out: ");
  Serial.println((VPORTC.IN & 0x08) != 0);
  counter = (counter + 1) & 0x7; // count modulo 8
  if (counter == 0) delay(1000);
}
```

The second example program *CCL2* uses Sequencer 0 in D flip-flop mode. The D input (LUT0) is connected to the sequencer output with an inversion so that it divides the LUT clock by two. The G input of the sequencer (LUT1) is connected to port pin PC0 and is toggled every millisecond. View the operation on an oscilloscope. The configuration in setup is:

```
CCL.LUT0CTRLB = CCL_INSEL0_FEEDBACK_gc; // Input from sequencer
CCL.TRUTH0 = 1; // Invert the input
CCL.SEQCTRL0 = CCL_SEQSEL0_DFF_gc; // D flipflop
CCL.LUT0CTRLA = CCL_OUTEN_bm | CCL_ENABLE_bm;
                // Enable with output enabled

CCL.LUT1CTRLB = CCL_INSEL0_IO_gc; // from I/O pin
VPORTC.DIR |= 1; // PC0 will control the D input
CCL.TRUTH1 = 0x2; // Pass through the input
CCL.LUT1CTRLA = CCL_ENABLE_bm; // Just turn it on

CCL.CTRLA = 1; // Enable the CCL
```

The loop function is:

```
void loop() {
  VPORTC.OUT |= 1; // Turn divider on
  delay(1);
  VPORTC.OUT &= ~1; // Turn divider off
  delay(1);
}
```

Here is the oscilloscope trace of the 8MHz generated output clock:

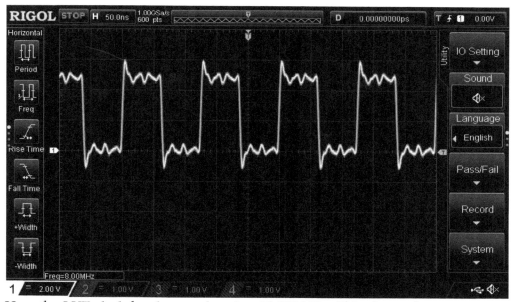

Here the LUT clock has been reduced to 32.768 kHz. This shows the gating every millisecond:

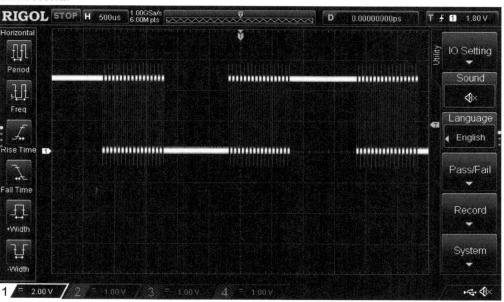

CHAPTER TWENTY-THREE

Clocks, Resets, Sleep Mode and Fuse Bits

As was mentioned in the USART section, the internal system clock is not very accurate. While it is factory calibrated at two supply voltages and both 16MHz and 20MHz frequencies, the resolution is such that there would still be too much error for proper USART operation. For this reason the factory calibration includes error variables that can be used for greater accuracy. Over the full operating range the frequency might be off by as much as 4%, although at nominal temperature and 3v ti would be within 1.5%,

The internal 32.768kHz oscillator can be off by as much as 20%, although at nominal temperature and 3v operation (they don't specify operation at 5 volts) it will be within 3%.

System Clock Speed

The Microchip documentation refers to a peripheral clock, CLK_PER. This is what I call the system clock. Devices that use asynchronous clocks, either the 16.384kHz clock or an external source, can sometimes also select the 16/20MHz clock directly as well. It is possible to select lower system clock speeds by using a divider off of the 16MHz or 20MHz oscillator.

Main Clock Control B Register CLKCTRL.MCLKCTRLB

Bit	7	6	5	4	3	2	1	0
Function				PDIV				PEN

The PEN bit enables the clock divider. PDIV selects the division factor:

Value	Description
0	/2
1	/4
2	/8
3	/16
4	/32
5	/64
8	/6
9	/10
10	/12
11	/24
12	/48

The register is protected with the Configuration Change Protection, which requires writing 0xD8 to register CPU_CCP immediately before writing to CLKCTRL.MCLKCTRLB. Note that this won't change the F_CPU value, which is determined when the microcontroller is booted up. So all time values will be generally off. See the example program *SLOW_CLOCK*.

The F_CPU value in the board.txt file can be changed to 8000000, 4000000, or 2000000 and the Arduino library code will set the CLKCTRL_MCLKCTRLB register appropriately for 8MHz, 4MHz, or 2MHz operation. If this is done then presumably all modules will work correctly. I say *presumably* because I haven't tested it and Arduino doesn't officially support operation at other than 16MHz. Changing the board.txt value will not work if BETTER_OPERATION or the 20MHz system clock is being used.

Resets

There are six sources that do a microcontroller reset:

- Power On Reset. This is automatic when the microcontroller VDD voltage rises to operating range.
- Brown Out Detector Reset. The Brown Out Detector can be configured to cause an interrupt when the power supply voltage drops below a certain point. If the voltage drops further the processor is reset. The Brown Out Detector is disabled by default on Arduino boards.
- Software Reset. The processor can be reset in software by first writing 0xD8 to register CPU_CCP and then immediately writing a "1" to register RSTCTRL.SWRR.
- External Reset. A low level on the RESET pin will reset the microcontroller as long as this feature is enabled by the RSTPINCFG bit in the SYSCFG0 fuse. The pin is enabled by default in the Arduino.
- Watchdog Reset. If the Watchdog timer is enabled, it can reset the microcontroller.
- Universal Program Debugger Interface Reset. The UPDI is the method used to program the Arduino Nano Every rather than using the bootloader. Since the UPDI is used, it is not necessary to have the External Reset enabled.

It is possible to determine the cause of the last reset by reading the RSTCTRL.RSTFR register.

Reset Flag Register RSTCTRL.RSTFR

Bit	7	6	5	4	3	2	1	0
Function			UPDIRF	SWRF	WDRF	EXTRF	BORF	PORF

UPDIRF - UPDI Reset occurred. SWRF - Software Reset occurred, WDRF - Watchdog Timer Reset occurred, EXTRF - External Reset occurred, BORF - Brownout Reset occurred, PORF - power on reset occurred. A power on reset sets PORF and resets all other flags. All flags can be cleared by writing "1" to them.

Sleep Mode

When selecting sleep mode, most peripherals can either run or be shut off depending on their RUNSTBY control bit. There is also a power down mode that basically shuts everything off but for some asynchronous inputs. If you wish to use a sleep mode to reduce power consumption you will need to read the Microchip documentation carefully.

The *SLEEP* demonstration program blinks the LED via the PIT interrupt, one cycle per second. The loop function toggles digital pin 2 and enters sleep mode. We can see how long the system sleeps by viewing pin 2 with an oscilloscope. The program turns off TCA0, and it's prescaler, which turns off all the Timer/Counters that rely on it.

When we do this we see that the microcontroller wakes twice a second to toggle the LED. If we don't turn off the TCA0 prescaler then interrupts occur once every 1.024ms to handle the TCB3 interrupt that keeps track of the time.

Fuse Bits

The fuse registers are written with every program download and three fuse registers are easy to modify because their values are specified in the boards.txt file. For instance, for the standard Arduino Nano Every there are lines nona4809.bootloader.*FUSEREGISTERNAME=value.*

nona4809.bootloader.SYSCFG0 (FUSE_SYSCFG0)

Bit	7	6	5	4	3	2	1	0
Function	CRCSRC				RSTPINCFG			EESAVE

The microcontroller is capable of performing a CRC check at power-up as a validity/security check. The default value CRCSRC=3 turns this feature off. RSTPINCFG is "1" for the reset pin to perform a reset and a "0" to be a GPIO pin. EESAVE is "1" to not erase the EEPROM as part of the chip erase (when programming) while "0" will erase the EEPROM. The default Arduino Nano Every value is 0xC9.

nona4809.bootloader.OSCCFG (FUSE_OSCCFG)

Bit	7	6	5	4	3	2	1	0
Function	OSCLOCK						FREQSEL	

OSCLOCK locks the 16/20 MHz oscillator calibration registers at run-time. You don't want to alter the calibration registers. FREQSEL selects the operating frequency. A value of 1 runs at 16MHz while a value of 2 runs at 20MHz. The default Arduino Nano Every value is 1.

nona4809.bootloader.BOOTEND (FUSE_BOOTEND)

This setting is used to reserve program memory for a boot loader. It should have a value of 0 in the Arduino Nano Every.

Other fuse registers are not readily accessible for change. They include WDTCFG and BODCFG to configure the Watchdog Timer and Brown Out Detector. These features can be configured in the setup function if desired. The register SYSCFG1 is used to set the startup time, the time the microcontroller waits after power on and before execution. It has a default value of 64ms, the maximum allowed. APPEND is used to set the end of application program memory and doesn't apply when BOOTEND=0. Finally LOCKBITS is used to lock the part. There is no way to read the contents of the memory externally (using the UPDI) when the part is locked. It may only be completely erased. By default the part is unlocked.

Source Code Available

Source code for all the examples can be downloaded from
https://almy.us/arduinoeverybook.html.

All the example programs can be freely distributed or used in applications with attribution.

References

The following links were tested to be active and correct at time of publishing.

Arduino website *http://arduino.cc*
Microchip documentation for AVR ATmega4809
       https://www.microchip.com/wwwproducts/en/ATMEGA4809
Wiring Project website *http://wiring.org.co*
AVR GCC website *https://gcc.gnu.org/wiki/avr-gcc*
AVR Libc website *https://www.nongnu.org/avr-libc*
Avrdude website *http://savannah.nongnu.org/projects/avrdude*